STUDENT TO FOUNDER

STUDENT TO FOUNDER

Secrets to creating a student organization in college
and starting a business after graduation

PATRICK D. GREENOUGH

Printed on demand. Location of physical printing depends on the geographic location of where the order originated.
First Edition, 2016
ISBN-13: 9780996290401
ISBN-10: 0996290400

PDG Projects
Los Angeles, CA / Albuquerque, NM
www.patrickgreenough.com

Cover design by: Tatiana Krasovski, www.illustratk.com
Editing by: Bobby Borg, Mary Curren, Marty Dall, Gregg Garcia, and Greg Imlay

TABLE OF CONTENTS

PREFACE

So why should you buy and read this book? Participating in student organizations at the college undergraduate, and graduate levels is an incredible way to gain valuable leadership and entrepreneurial skills. Even though this is such a valuable learning experience, it can be difficult to identify all the steps required to build a successful student organization.

Written by an experienced student and professional organization leader, Student to Founder is a helpful instructional guide meant to walk the reader through the process of starting, leading, and maintaining a successful student organization during the collegiate tenure. The methods provided in this manual can be applied to entrepreneurial efforts when starting a business.

This book is about the connection between academic leadership and professional entrepreneurship. The purpose is to teach college students how to practice being entrepreneurs by way of running successful student organizations. By doing this, they can better understand how the process works when they graduate and are ready to start businesses. This book brings clarity to this process.

Use this book to progress as a successful student leader and entrepreneur. It provides guidance to those inspired to take action to create their own success, to be role models, and make a lasting and positive impact on both their college and community.

NOTES WHILE READING:

* Look for mentions in footnotes about downloadable resources available at www.patrickgreenough.com/resources.
* Some of the key points are boldly stated in gray boxes. Keep an eye out for these; they are meant to stimulate thought.
* There are a variety of places in this book where lists of companies are referenced. Website URLs have been left off to prevent inaccuracies when or if URLs change. A simple Google search will reveal related information on respective brands.

PART I

Part I covers Networking Strategies, Team Formation, Recruiting, Paperwork, Programming, and Strategic Planning. Each of these concepts is covered in proprietary chapters called Secrets. Applications to entrepreneurship are considered in detail either within or in the concluding summary sections of each Secret.

Secret 1

NETWORKING AND ADDING VALUE

The academic environment is a great place to learn how to interact with diverse groups of people. It is also a safe place to make mistakes. This Secret begins with a discussion on effective networking strategies and concludes with a few points on prospecting and personal branding, and how they relate to business. The content in this Secret applies to student leaders and will show that to be successful, it is important to understand how to effectively interact with others. This is the core basis for gathering the right people to start an inaugural leadership team for your organization, or business.

1.1 NETWORKING

Networking is a great benefit of being a part of a student organization. You can learn a lot from your classmates. Take time to get to know them and see where it goes. You both might benefit from each other's skill sets, but you will never know until you begin interacting.

Sometimes, it is more about whom you know than what you know. Often the relationships we form lay the foundation for the success we create. Building relationships is critical to our success in business. Some of the greatest masterminds of our time created their success with the addition of a complimentary skill set from another person. For example, Steve Jobs built

Apple with Steve Wozniak. Each possessed unique skills that together allowed them to create a legendary company. Everyone has something, either skills or expertise that is valuable to someone else. The key is to find the people who have what you need. To do this, you need to identify where people spend their time and how they interact. Then you should frequent those locations and introduce yourself.

As a student, look for networking events that happen on your campus. Many universities and colleges maintain a public events calendar. If one exists at your institution, review it and plan to attend a few events. Make it a point to meet students from other areas of study. Your goal is to find people that either have skills you need for your objectives or who are connected to people who do. Focus on networking strategically.

While attending networking events, do not focus on acquiring business cards. Instead, focus on building sensible relationships with the right people. Focus on quality over quantity. If after a minute of talking with someone, you do not see any way that either of you can help each other, politely say goodbye and find someone else to interact with at the event. This is not a negative perspective, but it will allow you to focus on building the right kinds of relationships. Do not just gather business cards for the sake of gathering business cards. Acquiring just two business cards from people that possess complementary skill sets and a genuine interest in building a relationship with you is more productive than acquiring 50 business cards from people who do not. To slice a loaf of bread, it is much more efficient and effective to slice it with one sharp knife than it is to slice it with 50 spoons.

> To slice a loaf of bread, it's much more efficient and effective to slice it with one sharp knife than it is to slice it with 50 spoons.

While at networking events, think about how you introduce yourself to others. If you are an introvert, opening conversations might be uncomfortable. In this case, think of the stranger as someone who shares the same level of discomfort as you. You both may benefit from the introduction; it just takes one of you to break the ice. This can be a very gainful experience. Let's look at the various components of preparing and presenting your introduction.

SECRET 1: NETWORKING AND ADDING VALUE

1.1.1 DESIGNING YOUR BUSINESS CARD

I always carry a stack of business cards with me wherever I go. While I can very well just pull out my phone and plug information into my contact list, handing out a business card adds a physical touch point to the interaction. This is just another way to increase your chances of being remembered and you definitely want to be remembered.

If you are a current student, investigate if your school has branded business card templates for faculty, staff, and students. A good place to start is by contacting your Student Affairs/Activities Center.[1] These templates usually have the school's logo on them and options to include your full name, email, and phone number. Sometimes they will even allow spaces for field of study and anticipated graduation date.

If your school does not have a template, consider hiring a third party to make your cards. Design a business card consistent with the brand image you are trying to create for yourself, which will depend on your professional status. If you are a full-time student, you may want to use a conservative template with muted colors and a classic font such as Times New Roman. But then again, it is entirely up to you.

Create business cards that reflect your professional brand and keep a stack with you at all times. The card should include at least your full name and email address. You might also include your phone number, but I recommend against adding anything else to prevent it from looking too busy.[2]

When designing your business card, consider colors and fonts. The card should match your brand, whatever it may be. Be consistent with how you market your brand. You may not yet have a business, but you still have a personal brand. Think about how you want to market yourself to others. To better understand your personal brand, identify how you want to be seen.

If you attend school and run a business, identify a color and font combination consistent with your brand. To illustrate, if you sell motorcycles, you will likely not have a pink business card with a bright blue bubbly font. But

---

1 Student Affairs/Activities Center is covered in section 4.1.

2 The phone number adds another layer of distraction. If this concerns you, leave it off and only include your email address and/or links to social profiles. That way, you can be more in control of when and how you respond to incoming contact requests.

then again it depends on what kind of motorcycles you sell. Whatever the case, your business card should reflect your personal and professional brand and should be received well by your target audience. For student organizations, your target audience is made up of your current and prospective members. There are a variety of vendors that can print your business cards.

After you have a set of business cards made, keep stacks of them in places that you frequent the most, which might include your automobile's glove compartment, your backpack or briefcase, and your office. When you carry them with you, keep them in one of your jacket pockets and reserve the other jacket pocket for business cards acquired from other people. If you do not plan to wear a jacket, keep them in a front pocket somewhere, preferably shirt but pants are okay. It is highly encouraged not to put them in a back pocket of your pants. When you sit down, they get warm and may bend, which when handing them out may make you look unprofessional, unprepared, or worse. Keep your business cards in your front pockets, in jacket or shirt pockets if at all possible.

> Never put your own business cards in your back pocket.

1.1.2 PERFECTING YOUR HANDSHAKE

Perfecting your handshake is something that some may find intuitive, and others may find rather difficult; it just depends on your personality style. You want to make your introduction as memorable as possible while still maintaining strict professionalism. I like to state my full name and provide a firm, but not too firm, handshake. The firmness of the handshake is important but do not hurt the recipient's hand, or you may compromise the quality of your introduction. Grip the hand as hard as you would a handlebar during a normal bicycle ride. You should not be hanging on for dear life; just using it for its purpose, which is to keep you balanced on the bike.

Shake the person's hand while making eye contact and smiling. This will reduce anxiety and promote a welcoming introduction. It is also important to pay close attention to hand hygiene. Keep your finger nails trimmed and your hands clean as often as possible; you never know when or where you will meet someone so it will always work in your favor to be prepared. You might consider keeping a pair of nail clippers and a small bottle of hand sanitizer in your car, briefcase, or elsewhere close by for use when needed.

1.1.3 WEARING YOUR NAMETAG

If you find yourself in a situation where you are encouraged to wear a nametag, make note of placement. Your nametag should be placed on the same side of your jacket as your dominant hand used for the handshake. For example, if you are right handed, the nametag should be placed near or on your right shoulder. This allows the recipient of the handshake to keep your name and face in the same visual periphery. Matching a face to a name from the beginning is very important for memory, and you definitely want to be remembered.

1.1.4 CHOOSING YOUR WARDROBE

Always try to dress to match the occasion. You would not wear a tuxedo to a soccer game, and you also would not wear workout shorts to a wedding. Your wardrobe should always be context specific. Understand where you are going and dress for the occasion. All student organizations are different but when in doubt and unless you are the invited keynote speaker with specific wardrobe requirements, it almost always works in your favor to wear business casual attire. You should have a basic understanding of different professional ensembles so that you can be prepared to dress for any professional occasion. Figure 1.1 depicts a brief list of classic variations to consider when planning your ensemble. Gender specifics are provided where applicable.

The Casual	The Traditional	The Premier
Fitted, or Skinny Jeans	Fitted dress pants, skirt or dress	Fitted suit pants
Brown or black dress shoes for men; Neutral flats or heels for women	Brown or black dress shoes for men; Neutral flats for women	Brown or black dress shoes for men; Neutral heels for women
Brown or black belt: color of belt should match color of shoes	Brown or black belt: color of belt should match color of shoes	Brown or black belt: color of belt should match color of shoes
Untucked button-up collared shirt with top two buttons left unfastened	Tucked button-up collared shirt with top button left unfastened. Tie optional.	Tucked long sleeve button-up collared shirt with tie
Blazer unbuttoned	Sweater or vest buttoned	Suit jacket buttoned
Black dress socks for men	Black dress socks for men; Neutral stockings for women	Black dress socks for men

Figure 1.1: Appropriate Business Attire Options

1.1.5 IMPLEMENTING YOUR INTRODUCTION

Now that you look great, you have business cards that reflect your school or personal brand, and your nametag is placed on the same shoulder as your dominant hand, you are ready to shake hands and introduce yourself. Accompany the inaugural interaction with a question to stimulate conversation. Here is an example:

* *"Hi, my name is [insert your name here]. How are you?"*

Accompany that question with a smile and you are on your way. This question will help break the ice and allow each of you to get to know each other. Practice this enough times and it will become habitual.

When you discover the other person's name, try to use if at least five (5) times within the first few minutes of dialogue. This will help you remember the name. To improve his or her recall as well, try to use your own name at least five (5) times in conversation during that time. Here are some examples of things you can say:

* *"Hi [insert his or her name here], it's very nice to meet you."*
* *"[Insert his or her name here], what line of work do you practice?"*

*   *"So [insert his or her name here], tell me more about what you do?"*[3]
*   *"[Insert his or her name here], that reminds me of an event I hosted where my friend said to me, 'Hey [insert your name here], nice job planning this event; I've met some great people here.'…"*
*   *"Well, [insert his or her name here], it was very nice meeting you, and I look forward to connecting with you again in the future."*

Try to remain calm and collected during your interaction. Avoid sounding like you have memorized a script and aim to be authentic and genuinely interested in meeting that person. You might consider role-playing this with a friend a few times to help you polish your introduction.

1.2 PROSPECTING

Prospecting is an area that stems from networking. As mentioned in section 1.1.4, depending on the context, you should dress to fit the culture. The key to prospecting is fitting into the market. The first step is identifying your market and dressing for the occasion. If you run a student organization, you are looking for members of other groups with whom to collaborate, candidates to fill current or future officer roles, and inspiration for workshops or event concept ideas.

---

3 The "What do you do?" question is very traditional. From the modern standpoint, what people do may be different than how they make their money so a better question to ask is, "How do you make your money?"

SUMMARY AND APPLICATIONS TO ENTREPRENEURSHIP

So far, we have discussed the importance of dressing for the occasion and audience. We have touched on appearance, nametag placement, business card design, and even perfecting your handshake. By having an understanding of how to interact at networking events, you are in a better position to identify new opportunities. For the remainder of this Secret, we will discuss how to leverage your interactions at networking events to find new business. In business, three prospecting situations can be gained from networking, which include finding clients, identifying business partners, and securing jobs. Strategies for dealing with each of these methods are covered here.

1.2.1 FINDING NEW CLIENTS

If you are looking for new clients, you have to prepare yourself to attract them. This includes dressing for the occasion and acting in an inviting way. Be aware of the nature and atmosphere of the networking event. With regard to the other attendees, consider the following characteristics: age; appearance; and level of experience. Use this information to formulate tailored introductions. Your peers may enjoy a more casual introduction while seasoned professionals may require a more formal approach. The key is to consider the type of recipient of your introduction and plan accordingly. Strategically positioning your introduction improves your chances of finding new clients, and securing other profitable opportunities.

After you introduce yourself, carry the conversation by asking some simple but relevant questions. To promote the flow of conversation, these questions should be open-ended. Here are some examples:

* *"Tell me about the line of work you practice."*
* *"What does your company do in terms of [insert your craft here]?"*
* *"I work with companies in [subject area]. How does your team perform that function?"*

The idea is to ask questions that will reveal how and where you can fit into the equation. You want to let them know you are an expert at your craft, and you can share your expertise with them. Be modest with your communications but indicate specifically how you can provide a valuable service. Be intriguing without being pretentious.

Be true to yourself by not embellishing your abilities. Do not tell them you are a graphic designer when your only experience is using Microsoft Word to design a flyer for a garage sale. If you want more experience in a specific area, offer to give your aspiring skills away for free to gain experience and learn something new.[4] People love free work, so it is usually pretty easy to land free gigs to gain experience. Also, you will build valuable relationships that may potentially lead to additional free, or even paid work. Build trust first by offering free work. After trust has been formed, you should begin charging for your services. Be firm about these arrangements. It is unlikely that anyone will initiate a discussion about payments with you when they are already receiving your services for free. Create boundaries for yourself and commit to them. For example, you might offer a one-time complimentary service with any additional projects being paid services.

Let's continue using the graphic designer example. If you really are a seasoned graphic designer, know what you are worth and charge accordingly. If you are unsure of your value, research what others with comparable skill levels are charging and being paid. You might have to start at the bottom but do not undersell yourself. Make fair comparisons of your work with others. Once you have provided your skills for free, charge according to what the market is willing to bear.

1.2.2 IDENTIFYING YOUR VALUE

Your value is something you need to determine as early as possible. As stated earlier, if you are unsure of your professional value, conduct a quick market

---

4 Avoid being a long-term free work provider. Practice this strategy when looking to gain experience and do it only temporarily. If you have a talent, never give it away for free. Also, as the recipient of free work, accept that there is almost always a catch, which may not be immediately identifiable. This may include a future situation in which the provider expects you to return the favor in some way. This can get complicated very quickly. To avoid that, be sure to have an honest conversation with the free work provider about the terms of the work. This may include: start and end dates; workload; compensation potential for additional services rendered beyond the free work occurrence; and any other necessary expectations. Be sure to discuss the before, during, and after work delivery expectations, which should be clearly understood by both parties.

analysis to see what others are paying for similar services rendered. Couple this information with the following guideline:

Let's say it takes you 5 hours to complete a tri-fold marketing collateral piece; we will call a brochure. When your work is complete, compare the quality of your work with the quality of work done by established professionals who also design brochures. When you find comparable work done by someone else, contact that person and ask how much they charge to design a comparable brochure and also how long it takes them to complete the piece from start to finish. The trick is not to ask them as a competitor but to position the request as a customer. This will reduce the chances they will suspect you are conducting a competitor market analysis on price points.

Let's now say you find out the competitor is charging $1000 to design the brochure and it takes them approximately 10 hours to design from start to finish. This equates to $100 per hour of work completed.

As previously discussed, it takes you 5 hours to complete a brochure. If you feel your work is twice as superior to the competitors work and done at half the time, you can feasibly charge your clients twice as much as your competitor, which equates to $200 per hour. If your work is just marginally better, adjust this quote accordingly. This method will help you identify your value.

1.2.3 IDENTIFYING YOUR FEE STRUCTURE

There are two ways to charge for services rendered: per product, or per hour.

1.2.3.1 *Charging Per Product*

Charging per product can be tricky. It is very easy to think in per unit terms. While this is fine for standardized product lines, it is a little more ambiguous with different product requirements. If your clients all have the same product requirements, you could easily charge per product and not worry about much except for maybe updating a template with the requested information. If it takes you just a few minutes to revise a template, you could make use of the per product option. If on the other hand, your clients all have different requirements, it would be wiser to opt for the per hour option.

SECRET 1: NETWORKING AND ADDING VALUE

1.2.3.2 Charging Per Hour

Charging per hour is a more attractive option if your client portfolio makeup is widely diverse. One client might provide a series of objectives tied to a single deliverable. For example, the client might ask you to design a tri-fold collateral piece that may include a variety of design styles and image manipulations. In this case, it is best to opt for the hourly charge with a 1-hour minimum to cover you even if it actually takes less than one hour to complete. This helps keep the math simple. Unless the client asks, they do not need to know that it took you ten minutes to do an hour's worth of work. If the client does ask about duration, be honest but remind them that you have a 1-hour minimum charge. This is commonplace in business, and there is no need to apologize for an hour charge even if the deliverable took less time to complete.

1.2.4 FINDING NEW BUSINESS PARTNERS

Finding new business partners is similar to finding new clients but instead of looking for jobs from people, you are looking for people from jobs. After you gain some understanding of the quality and type of work that someone has done, you can begin to consider how your business objectives can benefit from his or her skill set.

1.2.5 FINDING WORK

For those who are less interested in entrepreneurship and more interested in finding full-time opportunities with already established companies, networking events can be very helpful. Getting face time with business executives can be a challenge. Sometimes they can be found at networking events, and you can capitalize on the opportunity. Be prepared to introduce yourself and tell them what type of position you are seeking.[5] The secret is to avoid being seen as needy. You can do this by creating a more collaborative atmosphere by what I like to call, *gold mining*.

---

5 For a discussion on how to implement your introduction, refer to section 1.1.5.

1.2.6 GOLD MINING

Gold miners spend their time digging through mud in hopes of finding bits and pieces of gold. Each piece of gold adds a little more value. In networking environments, you can be a gold miner by asking the other party questions in the hopes of uncovering information that reveals a need for your skill set. This is your digging time. Each question should be more refined than the last, and will reveal more information so keep digging! Let's look at an example of a series of questions and answers that showcase this structure. Your questions and their answers will vary, but this example will give you a better idea of how to be a gold miner in a networking situation.

MARK: *"So what project is your team working on at the moment?"*
JANE: *"We're building a website that integrates our latest technology for one of our newest clients."*
MARK: *"Oh wow! That sounds interesting. How many people do you have working on that?"*
JANE: *"We have two teams working on this particular initiative. Programming, and Marketing."*
MARK: *"Very nice! Tell me more about your marketing team. How many people are on it?"*
JANE: *"We currently have three people on the marketing team."*
MARK: *"How does each person on the marketing team work together?"*
JANE: *"They each have unique responsibilities. We have someone in market research, someone in advertising, and someone in sales."*
MARK: *"That's a nice combination. Who does your design work?"*
JANE: *"We don't have one specific person that does that. One person typically has an idea, and the three of them discuss it and then our advertising person drafts a design around it for review. It's usually a team effort."*
MARK: *"I actually work specifically in this area. I'm a graphic designer."*
JANE: *"Oh yeah? Very nice."*
MARK: *"Yeah, and I would love to provide another set of eyes on your next design piece. All you have to do is send me an email*

with a draft, and I'd be happy to have a look. No charge, what do you say?"

JANE: *"That sounds great. I think my team would appreciate that. I'll have someone from my marketing team reach out to you this week. Here's my card, send me a quick reminder tonight and I'll connect you this week."*

MARK: *"Excellent! Thank you. I look forward to working with your marketing team."*

In this example, Mark asked Jane a series of progressively refined questions. These questions led to a discussion that allowed Mark to gain an understanding of where his skills fit into the equation. Mark first identified a need and capitalized on that need by offering his skills for free. After Mark builds trust with Jane's team, he may consider creating a contractual agreement by acting as a consultant and charging for his services.[6]

1.2.7 OFFERING INSTEAD OF ASKING FOR VALUE

The example above illustrates how one person can find a growth opportunity in a networking situation. It is very important to structure your responses to show that your skills are seen as complementary to the objectives. Do not fake this. Only employ this strategy if it makes sense. Once the other party sees you are collaborative, it will almost always work in your favor. If you are collaborative instead of needy, you will have a stronger chance of being taken more seriously in future interactions with them. The take home point is to focus on adding value to others, not asking others to add value to you. Instead of asking for work, offer your skills to others and let them know you are interested in collaborating with them.

---

6 Be careful not to step on any toes when it comes to offering your services for free. While this can be helpful in the right circumstance, it's very possible to accidentally offend someone. In this case, it would be Jane or Jane's marketing team. Avoid making them feel incompetent. Use your best judgment during conversations and look for specific needs for your skill set before delivering the free offer.

Focus on giving value instead of asking for it.

In the above example, once Mark identified a need he offered his skills for free. This gave him an opportunity to earn Jane's trust. Once he proves himself with Jane's team, he is encouraged to charge for his services as a consultant.[7]

1.3 PERSONAL BRANDING

The content in this Secret has valuable implications to how we interact in business. To be perceived as a leader, you need to present yourself as a professional. This includes how to dress, how to talk, what to offer, and how to identify opportunities. All these factors relate to the concept of personal branding. Personal branding is the practice of marketing yourself as a brand. This includes marketing your persona and your career. Personal branding is integral to the development of your reputation, and your success. You should carefully select a wardrobe that is consistent with the brand that makes you the best version of yourself. Dress in a way that augments your confidence and allows you to present yourself and communicate with others in the most professional manner possible. You also want to position your communications in a tone-friendly way. You want to be seen as serious but inviting. This will help you attract people who may be influential.

1.4 BECOMING YOUR PEERS

Your success is also related to the alignment of your social network. Your network is contagious. If you want to be successful, you should interact with successful people. Take a look at your social network and ask yourself the following questions:

---

7 For a discussion on how to identify value and fee structure, refer to sections 1.2.2 and 1.2.3.

* Do any of these people motivate me to move forward in my career?
* Does the time I spend with these people help me grow personally or professionally?
* Can/do either of our skill sets complement each other?
* Do I look up to any of these people?
* Do I enjoy myself when I am around these people? (Be honest)

If you answered no to these questions, it might be time for you to revise your social network. Be selective about with whom you decide to spend your time. Our social groups are very influential to our personal and professional growth and development. Care should be taken when building new relationships because time is finite and the relationship should make sense to both of you. If you each have something to offer one another in terms of personal or professional growth, that relationship may be desirable. Otherwise, you may want to reconsider. Be aware and choose your contacts and friends wisely.

If you want to be successful, get to know successful people.

Secret 2

SCOUTING TALENT AND FORMING A TEAM

This Secret focuses on strategies for identifying potential candidates to fill officer positions for your student organization. In this Secret, we will discuss the personality characteristics and skill sets to identify in others to construct an effective team.

2.1 IDENTIFYING YOUR SKILL SET

Identifying your skill set is the first step in team formation. Before you can identify the skills you need, you must first understand the skills you have. This requires introspection and self-awareness. You need to be honest and true to yourself. Look objectively at what you can and cannot do. For example, you might be great at crunching numbers but not so great at managing money. In this case, financial management may not be your strongest quality, but you might excel in another area, such as accounting. The point is to accept the level of strength you possess in each of your skills. Whatever skills you lack are skills you need to find in others.

As the word denotes, 'team' is made up of more than one person. You cannot expect to do everything yourself when you belong to a team. It is neither expected nor desired. To augment process efficiency, required skills must be effectively divided among the various team members. You can create a cooperative symbiotic unit by selecting the right individuals to become team members.

Each of us has a variety of skills, some more valuable than others. The key is to identify which skills are relevant to your organization. To do this, you must first define what skills your organization requires. If you want your student organization to remain stable over time, you must run it like a business and expect or aim to fill specific roles in your organization.

Run your student organization like a business.

2.2 IDENTIFYING OFFICER ROLES

Student organization leaders have complete freedom over what roles to fill in their executive committees. The following is a list of commonly required roles for a student organization to operate productively. Each role is coupled with implications for common skill sets and personality characteristics required to optimally accommodate the respective responsibilities. For these descriptions and to better understand personality requirements, a possible Myers-Briggs personality type is assigned to each of the officer roles.[1]

2.2.1 BOARD ADVISOR:

This person is not technically an officer, but is typically required, if not at least strongly encouraged to be part of the organization in the academic environment. The person in this role is usually a faculty member within a subject area relevant to the organization and acts as the director of the organization. This person may provide the President with steering assistance in executive level decisions.

---

1 Profiles of the Sixteen Personality Types. (n.d.). Retrieved April 20, 2016, from http://www.truity.com.

* Skills and Personality: Exceptionally proficient leader, and communicator. Interested in the executive advancement of the organization.
* Possible Myers-Briggs personality type: ESTJ or ENFJ

2.2.2 PRESIDENT:

This officer oversees all active board members. This includes all Vice President's (VPs), the Secretary, and the Treasurer. This person is the leader of the group and maintains communications with the Board Advisor.

* Skills and Personality: Can combine both leadership and management skills, think globally, and solve complex problems.
* Possible Myers-Briggs personality type: ESTJ

2.2.3 SECRETARY:

This officer is responsible for recording minutes during officer meetings, and managing appointments when necessary. Some organizations title this role as VP Records.

* Skills and Personality: Detail-oriented, active listener, and practical solution investigator.
* Possible Myers-Briggs personality type: ISTP

2.2.4 TREASURER:

This officer is responsible for managing the financial assets and liabilities of the organization. This includes drafting regular Profit & Loss (P&L) Statements, and Balance Sheets. Some organizations title this role as VP Finance or VP Accounting.

* Skills and Personality: Interested in maintaining order and organization, detail-orientated, trust, analytics, and methods.
* Possible Myers-Briggs personality type: ISTJ

2.2.5 VICE PRESIDENT (VP) POSITIONS:

These officers oversee specific areas of the chapter. To prepare for succession planning, each of these officers should train and oversee a volunteer or committee of volunteers to help complete tasks.[2]

2.2.5.1 *VP Collegiate Relations:*

This officer manages strategic relationships with student organizations from either his or her own or from other colleges and/or universities. This role is important when planning joint events. If this role is done at the professional level, this person could form a committee made up of brand ambassadors from each college and/or university.

* Skills and Personality: Extrovert, social, organized, and managerial.
* Possible Myers-Briggs personality type: ENFJ

2.2.5.2 *VP Communications:*

This officer handles correspondences with current and prospective members. This includes managing all responsibilities pertaining to newsletters, emails, social media and any other forms of notification.

* Skills and Personality: Extrovert, social, and articulate.
* Possible Myers-Briggs personality type: ENFJ

2.2.5.3 *VP Marketing:*

This officer manages efforts related to service demand. Possible responsibilities include designing the organization logo, marketing collateral, and finding ways to increase brand awareness and market demand.[3]

---

2 Succession planning is covered in section 6.3.

3 Marketing strategies are covered in Secret 9.

* Skills and Personality: Creative, entrepreneurial, and forward thinking.
* Possible Myers-Briggs personality type: ENTP

2.2.5.4 VP Membership:

This officer is responsible for membership growth. This may include managing retention of existing members and identifying opportunity areas for recruiting new members. This officer may also conduct classroom pitches.[4]

* Skills and Personality: Creative, detail-oriented, social, and interested in building new and strengthening existing relationships.
* Possible Myers-Briggs personality type: ENFP

2.2.5.5 VP Programming:

This officer is responsible for event planning. This includes prospecting to secure venues and designing event concepts.[5]

* Skills and Personality: Organizational, social, detail-oriented, and creative.
* Possible Myers-Briggs personality type: ENTJ

2.2.5.6 VP Sponsorship:

This officer is responsible for partnership acquisitions. This includes finding businesses to collaborate with on initiatives where both parties may benefit. This is a sales role.[6]

* Skills and Personality: Business development, relationship management, and socially refined.
* Possible Myers-Briggs personality type: ESTP

---

4 Pitching to classrooms is covered in section 3.1.
5 Programming strategies are covered in Secret 5.
6 Partnership development strategies are covered in Secret 5.

SECRET 2: SCOUTING TALENT AND FORMING A TEAM

2.2.5.7 VP Technology:

This officer is responsible for managing and overseeing all initiatives related to the website. This includes building, designing, updating, troubleshooting, and maintaining the security of the website.[7]

* Skills and Personality: Technical, detail-oriented, problem solving, and creative.
* Possible Myers-Briggs personality type: INTJ

The above set of officer titles illustrates some of the necessary parts required to make up an effective and efficient team. Your organization might have more, fewer, or different officer positions depending on the number of members and desired management responsibilities. Additionally, if one responsibility becomes too cumbersome for a single person, you can always create co-position opportunities where more than one person holds the same title, i.e., Co-VP Communications, etc. This will help better distribute some of the responsibilities. A lot of work can be delegated to committee members as well, which is typically encouraged to facilitate the development of managerial skills.

2.3 MANAGING DELEGATION AND VOLUNTEERS

2.3.1 OPTIMAL DELEGATION:

To ensure that information and tasks flow efficiently through your resources, it is important to delegate work to the proper board member(s) or volunteer(s). Communicate this expectation with your board so they know to whom they should pass information and why. For example, let's say that you are the VP of Technology, and your job is strictly website related. You have been sent an email by a sponsor inquiring about the possibility of sending your members a proprietary newsletter about an event. You should do one of two things:

---

7 Website creation strategies are covered in Secret 10.

1. Forward the email to your VP of Communications and politely invite them to respond to the sponsor
2. Cc the VP of Communications in your reply to the sponsor and make an introduction to both

This strategy goes both ways. If the VP of Communications receives an inquiry about the website, it should be forwarded to you if you are the VP of Technology. Try to be as accurate as possible when delegating tasks and make sure everyone on your team takes complete ownership and accountability for their roles.

2.3.2 VOLUNTEERS:

Depending on the size of your audience and number of officers you have, you will likely receive interest from potential or active members that want to provide their skills to benefit your organization in some way. These people are called volunteers. Having volunteers is just as important as managing them. It is common for members or non-members to recommend some idea related to the general advancement of your organization. The best way to handle this without affecting your bandwidth[8] is to invite that person to manage and carry out his or her idea(s) on his or her own. This creates ownership and makes the idea implementation process more efficient. If a relevant committee exists, consider introducing that person to the respective committee members.

Don't focus on working more; focus on working more efficiently.

2.4 FILLING OFFICER POSITIONS

When filling officer positions, focus on personal growth and professional development. That may mean you need to put yourself in uncomfortable

---

8 Bandwidth can be defined as the maximum amount of mental capacity or project process one person or team can manage at once. The more capacity or process that's managed, the thinner the bandwidth becomes, which can lead to inefficient and/or inadequate performance.

situations. Sometimes the best way to learn to swim is to just jump in the water. That is, learn by doing. While doing this may be potentially stressful for some, it is a great way to force one to learn and develop new and existing skills. This situation applies to various phases of organizational development. Let's have a look at specific phases where this method would apply.

2.4.1 IMPLEMENTING INAUGURAL OFFICER POSITION FULFILLMENT

When you first begin forming your organization, if you are the only person involved, by default you will be the President of the organization. In this case, it will be your responsibility to find people to fill the necessary roles for the executive team. During the inaugural process, you should be more focused on personality-job fit when filling officer positions.[9] Here is a list of possible opportunities where you might meet potential candidates to fill these roles:

* **Academic Networking Events:** These are great opportunities to meet likeminded classmates. Typically the types of people that attend these events are looking to further themselves in some way professionally, so you have a good chance of finding individuals that possess the specific characteristics that make effective officers. Review your school newspapers and event bulletin boards to search for events related to the subject of your organization. If your organization caters to business students, find events that these folks might be attending.[10]
* **Class Rosters:** Meeting people in class should be very easy to do. Given all of the often-required group projects and presentations, the classroom environment is a great place to learn to interact with and meet new people.
* **Casual Encounters:** This may also be relatively painless depending on the size of your school and the concentration of your student body. If you are outgoing, introducing yourself to other students may be easy to do. If

---

9 For examples of roles and personalities, refer to section 2.2.
10 For a detailed review of networking strategies, refer to Secret 1.

this is tougher for you, try to convince yourself that the recipient is just as nervous as you are. This will help you feel less stressed about initiating the inaugural encounter. Depending on the size of your school, you may want to strategically place yourself in specific locations. For example, if your organization is associated with the business school, it would make more sense to be seen there than in the college of the arts. You are more likely to find the right candidates in the right context and location.

2.4.2 IMPLEMENTING SEASONED OFFICER POSITION FULFILLMENT

Handling officer turnover when your organization is already established differs from the inaugural process. As indicated previously, during the inaugural process, you should be more focused on personality-job fit when filling officer positions. Over time, the focus should transition to developing your remaining officers. Term-to-term, you should encourage officers to entertain other positions with the intention and interest to learn new skills. Holding various officer positions over the course of your leadership tenure will allow you to learn how to manage other aspects of the organization. This process will make you a well-rounded leader, and will serve you well later when you run a business.

If you are majoring in Marketing, it makes sense to be interested in the VP Marketing position. You might make a fine Marketing VP given your mastery of the subject area. After a term, you might consider transitioning into something opposite of Marketing, like Accounting. If your organization has a VP position in this area, you may want to consider transitioning into it to gain a better understanding of the respective area. This is a great opportunity to learn something new and become more competitive as both an applicant and as an entrepreneur.

2.5 EXTENDING THE INVITATION

Extending the invitation is specific to the development of your inaugural executive team. Since you are the founder of this organization, you are free to manage it however you wish. While you may have a formal election process right out of the gate, it is typically not necessary when you are creating something entirely new. In this case, gathering your team is a more informal process and much like an invitation.

Be careful not to let general excitement influence the decision-making process. Give yourself a chance to get to know individuals before inviting them to be officers of your new organization. To avoid the premature invitation and strengthen the reassurance of the quality of the prospect, invite individuals to attend your meetings. You want to learn more about their behavior during meetings.

2.5.1 ASKING QUESTIONS ABOUT EVENT ATTENDEES

At your first meeting, think about the following questions regarding each attendee. This will help you better identify potential candidates to fill your inaugural officer roster. Each question is coupled with reasons why it is necessary to consider.

* **How are they interacting with other people in the room?**
  o The frequency and quality of interactions will help you gauge his or her social aptitude. It will also help you gauge how welcoming they are to others.
* **Are they asking questions, and if so how relevant are those questions?**
  o This will help you gain an understanding of his or her thought processes and degree of curiosity. It might also provide some insight on his or her ability to think critically.
* **How do they present themselves?**
  o This has to do with the two Ds: dress and demeanor. Individuals who take themselves more seriously will care about how they present themselves to promote an image of professionalism.[11]

---

11 For a review of appropriate business attire options, refer to section 1.1.4.

* **Do you have their full attention?**
  ○ In a world where digital technology is integrated into almost every interaction, it is important to find people who are not easily distracted by screens. Pay close attention to attendees that are fully engaged in your physical presentation.
* **What skills do they have, and are any of them relevant to any of your officer responsibilities?**
  ○ An understanding of skills can be achieved by allowing everyone in the room to introduce themselves and tell the rest of the group a little bit about why they are interested in your organization, what they hope to get out of it, and how they intend to contribute to it. Not only will this allow you to determine who can do what, but it will also allow the other attendees to better understand who they want to get to know. This will naturally stimulate the possibility of group formation. These groups can make great committees that can be overseen by specific VPs when chosen.

SUMMARY AND APPLICATIONS TO ENTREPRENEURSHIP
2.6 IDENTIFYING YOUR RESOURCE NEEDS

To understand what you need, you need to first understand what you have. When forming a student organization, you need to identify skills that you do not already have. Others should provide those. The others you choose will make up your executive team. It is important to allow yourself some time to get to know potential candidates first before inviting them to fill officer roles.

The implications to entrepreneurship can be applied directly to the concept of human resources. When you conduct a candidate search for your business, you will evaluate the degree of personality-job fit and how it relates to the compatibility between the candidate's skill set and your working objectives. If upon review of the candidate's professional background you find there could be a possible match, invite the candidate to either apply for the position or if they have already applied invite them in for an interview.

2.7 ACQUIRING TALENT

The interview process is a great opportunity for you to ask specific questions about the candidate's work history. Candidate answers provide valuable insights about them. Let's look at some examples of interview questions you might consider asking during candidate interviews. Look for candidates who interview you during this process. That is a clear indication of their self-awareness and interest in personality-job fit.

The following is a list of questions that you may consider asking potential team members.

* **"Tell me about yourself."** This may be one of the most common questions. Look for answers that indicate relevance to core objectives. Top candidates will talk less about where they grew up and more about how his or her skill sets can help grow your organization.
* **"If offered to you, what do you plan to get from this opportunity?"** This can be a tricky one for candidates because it immediately puts their wants and needs into question. Top candidates will

emphasize how their personal and professional goals will complement and enrich the strategic goals of the organization.

* **"Tell me about a time when you experienced a setback and what you did to overcome it."** Look for a response that indicates a clear example and how the candidate learned from the setback. The severity of the setback is less important than the lesson learned from it. Top candidates will be able to demonstrate humility and articulate knowledge transfer.

The process of identifying talent to lead your student organization has many implications to identifying quality employees to run your business. Much the same types of situations occur in both arenas. Practicing these methods at the collegiate level will help you develop highly desirable talent acquisition skills, which will be useful when you run your own business.

Secret 3

RECRUITING MEMBERS

Recruitment is critical to the growth and sustainability of your student organization. The concept of marketing will be discussed more specifically later. In this Secret, we will cover a strategic method for marketing your student organization directly to students via the classroom pitch.

3.1 PITCHING TO CLASSROOMS

This is a form of direct marketing and a great way to inform students of your organization. This method requires the ability to speak comfortably in front of classrooms of all sizes. When you schedule these pitches, decide which of your executive leaders will be implementing them. The classroom pitch is an opportunity to strengthen your comfort level with public speaking. If this intimidates you, you might consider doing it for the sake of practice. You will be surprised at how quickly you will become comfortable. Here are some specifics for planning these pitches.

3.1.1 IDENTIFYING YOUR TARGET MARKET

You want to sell your student organization to the right market. It has to make sense. If your organization is about marketing, you want to make your pitch in marketing and other business classes. If your organization is about art, you want to make your pitch in art, theater, or related classes. After you determine where you want your message to be heard, contact the instructors and/or professors of those targeted classes. This process is simplified if you already know the instructors and/or professors.

3.1.2 BUILDING RAPPORT WITH FACULTY

It is very necessary and important to build rapport with instructors and professors as early as possible during your academic tenure. Having strong relationships with these professionals greatly improves the success rate of a presentation request. If you do not have relationships with any instructors and/or professors, it is never too late to begin building them. Even if you do not have the rapport but still wish to make a pitch, you should go ahead and make the request. Most instructors and professors want their students to succeed so these requests are almost always welcomed.[1]

3.1.3 POSITIONING YOUR REQUEST

Inviting yourself to pitch to a classroom of students should be strategic in nature, but it does not have to be difficult. Email is the easiest and the often most productive way to begin. The email request allows you to carefully structure and review the request for accuracy, tone, and completeness. Once you create an acceptable draft, you can use it as a template for future requests. See Figure 3.1 for an example of an email to send to an instructor or professor to request an opportunity to make a brief pitch in his or her classroom.[2]

---

1 In the few instances that I was unable to secure a presentation, it was because the professor didn't reply to my emails. If this happens, keep searching for other opportunities.

2 Download the FREE template at https://www.patrickgreenough.com/resources.

"Dear [Prefix. Last name of instructor or professor],

I hope this message finds you well. I really enjoyed your course on [subject]. Your lectures were both insightful and entertaining, and I look forward to applying this knowledge to my professional endeavors.

I am contacting you to see if you would be willing to do something for me. I am the founder and president of a new student organization here on campus called, [name of organization]. This organization is valuable to students in that [reason why it is valuable to students]. In an effort to build awareness of my organization, I am scheduling brief 5-minute classroom presentations in select classes during the first two weeks of school this coming semester. Would you be willing to allow me to share a few words about my organization with your students during that time?

Thank you in advance for your consideration. I look forward to hearing from you.

Regards,
[Your full name]"

Figure 3.1: Classroom Pitch Email Template

Notice the flow of the above message. The message is made up of two parts: Acknowledgment and Request.

Part I: Acknowledgement

The message starts as an acknowledgement of your perception of his or her positive impact on your future. This is a nice touch and helps attract attention to the message. It also helps retain an interest in the rest of the message. Typically when you make a request, it is highly encouraged to acknowledge the recipient in some way. There are two situations in which you can position your acknowledgement:

1. **When the recipient has done something for you previously:** By thanking the recipient for what they did for you previously, you are reminding them of how valuable they are or have been to you.
2. **When the recipient has not done something for you previously:** If this is your first request for something from the recipient, let them know why you selected them to make this request. Indicate why they are so important to your initiatives.

Part II: Request

The second portion of the message should be relatively direct. You want to state only the necessary information. This includes stating your organizational title, the name of your organization, why it is beneficial to students, and your specific request. End the message with a question to help stimulate an immediate reply.

If you do not receive a response within a few days, send a follow-up reminder. While it is discouraged to send the same message again, you should consider sending some variation of it so they are aware you are still interested in hearing from them.

3.1.4 IMPLEMENTING THE PITCH

Once the instructor or professor has accepted your request, you are ready to plan your pitch. The structure of the pitch should be very straightforward, and last only five minutes. The content of the pitch should include the following:

* **Who:** Present your full name and organizational title
  o Descriptive.
* **What:** State the name of your organization
  o Descriptive.
* **Why:** Explain why students should join
  o Be as direct as you can here. Inform the students why their membership will be valuable to them. Let them know about some of the projects and activities you have planned. Focus on adding value.
* **When:** Share the when and where of your first meeting
  o Before you speak, look behind you and see if there is a white board or chalkboard available. If so, write down the following information. Look for high contrast color markers or chalk. When possible, use a black dry erase marker, or white chalk. It would be wise to bring the marker and chalk with you in the unlikely event that these items are not supplied.

<u>What to Write on the White Board or Blackboard:</u>

* **What:** [The name of your organization] Inaugural meeting
* **Where:** Building name, and room number
* **When:** Date, and time

Write the above information off to the side if the board is behind you so that you are not standing directly in front of it when you are talking. This information will act as an accompaniment to your pitch. Do not erase this information when you are finished with your pitch. Hopefully, it will remain on the board after you leave the classroom so that students can continue to observe it.

Try to be as direct and brief as possible when giving your presentation. There is no need to tell stories. This is your opportunity to make a quick but effective first impression. Be professional. Remember, you are using class time so make it valuable. The duration of your presentation should not exceed five minutes.

3.1.5 CAPTURING CONTACT INFORMATION WITH A SIGN-IN SHEET

After you have pitched your presentation, hand around a sheet of paper requesting names, phone numbers, and emails. It is wise to prepare a sign-in sheet with these headings in advance. People are more inclined to voluntarily donate this information when it is specifically requested in print. This will help you build your email list for marketing communications. Figure 3.2 was created in Microsoft Excel and represents an example of how your sign-in sheet could look.[3]

---

3 Download the FREE template at https://www.patrickgreenough.com/resources.

[YOUR LOGO HERE]				
			Yes	No
Full Name	Email Address	Phone Number	Member	

Figure 3.2: Event Sign-In Sheet

Notice how the sheet has columns for member and non-member identification. Each of these groups is different and should be marketed to uniquely. For revived or matured organizations, this distinction should be made. For newly formed organizations, this distinction will not be made until your organization reaches maturation over the course of time, so your sign-in sheet does not need these columns.

Phone numbers should be used sparingly and with the strict intention to reach out to uninvolved members to re-stimulate interest in the organization. Say, for example, you have 400 members, and 100 of them are inactive. You could invite your volunteer(s) to call the 100 inactive members to remind them of the value of your organization and their participation. This is also a nice opportunity to market your next event. The phone call follow-up is a great touch point and allows you to build new, and strengthen existing relationships with your members. A phone call follow-up should be done as a batch once a year. Make all of those 100 calls in a single session and be done with it until the next year.[4] Be courteous without being pushy.

Come prepared with several copies of your sign-in sheet and pass the stack around secured to a clipboard with a pen. It is important to pass this around only after you have finished your pitch. Before you get up to speak, take a look at the structure of the classroom and identify the best place to start passing around the clipboard. Your goal is to pass it around in such a way that it ends up closest to the door so that you can wait there and make a clean, quiet exit when the clipboard reaches you. To be sure this happens, inform the students where you will be sitting and ask them to pass the clipboard around so that it ends up back in your possession.

---

4 Apply this strategy when including phone numbers in voicemails: state your full name and phone number before saying anything else; and restate both again after you've verbalized your message. This will improve recall and save the recipient time if they need to hear your phone number again. By including your phone number at the beginning of the voicemail and not just at the end, the recipient will only need to re-listen to a fraction of the total voicemail should they need to hear the phone number again.

SUMMARY AND APPLICATIONS TO ENTREPRENEURSHIP

Direct marketing occurs when you market your services straight to the end customer. In the case of student organizations, direct marketing occurs when you market directly to students. After you have identified your target market, approach instructors and/or professors to request approval for a five-minute pitch at the beginning of their classes. Consider how best to structure your request in an email message, which will vary depending on whether or not they have helped you with something in the past. After you get approval, make your presentation brief and to the point. The only information you need to share is your name and title, the name of your organization, why it is valuable to join, and when and where the first meeting will take place. After which, you will hand out a sign-in sheet requesting name, phone number, and email address to be used for marketing communications.

3.2 IDENTIFYING YOUR TARGET MARKET

This Secret focuses on the process of identifying your target audience. In school, you are looking for students who may have an interest in interacting with your organization. It is the same in business; only instead of looking for students to join your organization, you are looking for customers to buy your product or service. It is important to acknowledge the difference between product-centric marketing, and customer-centric marketing. Product-centric marketing pertains to the product or service while customer-centric marketing pertains to the customer. If you are selling a product, you should investigate the market demand for that product before you spend your marketing dollars. Identify what your customers are doing and see if there is a missed opportunity somewhere. If you find an opportunity, and it complements your product or service, there may be a market demand for your product or service.

A review of the demographics of your target audience can reveal insights about what characteristics increase the likelihood of consumer spending. If you find untapped customers that also possess these characteristics and interests, you may be able to expand your market reach. When generating new business, focus on building relationships within the market instead of actively pushing your product into the market.

3.3 SEGMENTING YOUR MARKET

Demographics and psychographics should be considered to better understand and further define your target market.[5]

3.3.1 REVIEWING DEMOGRAPHICS

Demographics are the quantitative statistics of a population. You should consider researching the demographics of your target market. Some common demographics and associated questions include the following:

* **Age.** What is the average age or age range?
* **Gender.** What is the ratio of men to women?
* **Race.** What is the nationality makeup?
* **Education.** What is the range of education?
* **Location.** Where do they live and are their homes rented or owned?
* **Income.** How much do they make per year?
* **Occupation.** How do they make their money?
* **Marital status.** What is the ratio of single to married?

Understanding your customer demographics will greatly improve the effectiveness of your product or service offerings. For example, if your product is designed specifically for graduating seniors, you might ensure that your website showcases content such as graduate school reviews, interview tips, and professional wardrobe advice. This is just one of many examples of how you can revise your offerings to better accommodate your target audience.[6]

3.3.2 REVIEWING PSYCHOGRAPHICS

Psychographics are statistics related to qualitative characteristics of your target marketing. Some common psychographics and associated questions could include the following:

---

5 Porta, M. (2009, March 3). How to Define Your Target Market. Retrieved April 20, 2016, from http://www.successdesigns.net.

6 To learn more about demographics of a particular area, visit the U.S. Census Bureau website.

*   **Hobbies.** How do they spend their free time?
*   **Interests.** What do they like to talk about?
*   **Religious beliefs.** What denomination is most prominent if any?
*   **Lifestyles.** How do they live?
*   **Values.** What is most important to them?
*   **Opinions & Attitudes.** What do they think about certain topics?
*   **Personalities.** How do they socialize?

Researching psychographics will help you better understand the personality makeup of your target audience. You can use this information to further refine your offerings to accommodate these characteristics.

3.4 RESEARCHING YOUR MARKET

Identifying the psychographics of any target market requires deep research that may occur via longitudinal studies conducted over a series of months or even years. Here are some tips to help you conduct your research.

3.4.1 SAMPLING YOUR POPULATION

Your population sample size is very important for revealing accurate and generalizable information. Your sample size should be at least 30 for results to be statistically generalizable.[7] The larger your sample size, the more normally distributed your data will become. This is known as the Central Limit Theorem.[8] Keep this in mind when sampling a population randomly to better understand the psychographics of your target market.

3.5 INTERACTING WITH YOUR MARKET

If your product or service pertains to a specific industry, you should find unique ways to market to customers within that industry. Match your product

---

7 A sample size of 30 is generally considered the minimum required to achieve statistical significance.
8 Paret, M., & Martz, E. (2009, August). Tumbling Dice & Birthdays Understanding the Central Limit Theorem - Minitab. Retrieved April 20, 2016, from https://www.minitab.com.

or service offerings to those market vendors that have an existing inventory of items within your product category. If you want to be bold, reach out to vendors that do not yet, but could possibly benefit from carrying an inventory of your product(s).

As discussed in section 3.1.2, if you already know the person to whom you are reaching out, it smoothens the interaction and improves your chances of securing a desirable marketing arrangement for your product or service. Start with your own network first and see if you can identify anyone who does business in the industry to which you are trying to market. If you cannot identify anyone, look for referral opportunities. You will need to do a bit of initial legwork in the form of networking to ensure you get in contact with the right people.[9]

Before you reach out to potential vendors, write out a list of features pertaining to your product or service. Then list the benefits that each feature provides. For instance, an automobile break-pad manufacturer might state their new pads help improve the performance and, in addition, help improve overall safety. This is actually a double benefit, which is even more desirable. Once your benefits list is created, identify and market to customers who have a need for the benefits that your product or service fulfills.

3.6 ANALYZING THE COMPETITIVE ENVIRONMENT

Whether you are starting a student organization or starting a business, you should always conduct a competitor analysis first. Identify if something already exists in the market that meets the needs of your target market. If one does, consider revising your scope to offer something different, and avoid the potential of a market redundancy. While there is nothing wrong with direct competition, it is harder to capture an audience whose needs are already being accommodated elsewhere. Keep an eye on the competition without mimicking it.

---

9 For a review of networking strategies, refer to Secret 1.

Business is about monetizing a unique accommodation for an identified market need (Ideally with a market share that is not yet captured).

Once you have investigated the competitive environment, create a list of your competitors. Next to each competitor, write a list of each of the following characteristics for each one: strengths; weaknesses; opportunities; and threats. This is known as a SWOT Analysis.[10] See Figure 3.3.

STRENGTHS Internal | Positive - Can Control -	← CONVERT Weaknesses to Strengths ←	WEAKNESSES Internal | Negative - Can Control -
↑ MATCH Strengths with Opportunities ↓		
OPPORTUNITIES External | Positive - Can't Control -	← CONVERT Threats to Opportunities ←	THREATS External | Negative - Can't Control -

Figure 3.3: SWOT Analysis

The four components of the SWOT Analysis are defined as follows:

* **Strengths (S):** Core competencies that allow for a competitive advantage. These are internal factors, which can be controlled. Strengths may include rich financial resources, strong employee commitment, and an extensive product portfolio.
* **Weaknesses (W):** Any limitations that exist due to lack of skills or other resources. These are internal factors, which can be controlled.

---

10 SWOT Analysis - Definition, Advantages and Limitations. (n.d.). Retrieved April 20, 2016, from http://www.managementstudyguide.com.

Weaknesses may include antiquated technology, lack or resources, and small product portfolio.

* **Opportunities (O):** Market conditions that provide opportunities to further enhance existing strengths. These are external factors, which cannot be controlled. Opportunities may include the lifting of limitations posed by deregulation, new legislation, and a change in market competition.

* **Threats (T):** Circumstances or conditions that prevent growth and development. These are external factors, which cannot be controlled. Threats may include weak or weakened employee loyalty, and increased competition.

The SWOT Analysis can be used to determine optimal resource allocation strategies. Depending on available resources, you may only be able to focus on improving either strengths or identifying additional opportunities. Circumstance will influence where and when resources should be applied.

SWOT Analysis in Action:
This example will explain how each of these components can be applied. While this discussion will not cover complex topics such as profit margins, sales volume, and gross and net revenues, your team should discuss these items in detail.

Let's say it is a hot summer day and I run a cold drink stand in my neighborhood. Currently, I only sell lemonade from concentrate at $0.50 a cup. There is one competitor in the neighborhood that sells fresh squeezed orange juice at $0.75 a cup, and grape juice popsicles for the same price.

* **Strengths:** I offer a unique product from that of my competitor, and I sell it at a better price.

* **Weakness:** The quality of my product is inferior to my competitor; my lemonade is from concentrate while the orange juice offered by my competitor is fresh squeezed. Another weakness is I only carry a single product while my competitor has a multi-product portfolio.

* **Opportunities:** I should begin offering fresh squeezed orange juice or change my lemonade product from concentrate to the fresh squeezed

variety. I should also consider extending my menu to include other cold treats.
*   **Threats:** The competitor offers a higher quality, multi-category product line.

In this example, I would see the grape juice Popsicle as an indication to also carry cold treats at my stand. Instead of carrying grape popsicles, however, I could carry a variety of ice cream products, and in doing so own a product category in my region. Additionally, if I changed my juice format from concentrate to fresh squeezed, and offered juice from a different or higher quality fruit, I would offer a unique product line instead of emulating my competitor. If I take actions to identify and implement opportunities such as these, my summer time refreshment stand would become more competitive and profitable.

You should aim to identify and routinely observe your competitors. This will help you refine your service or product offerings and allow you to develop your core identity. Once you have identified your place in the market, aim to maintain that position by continually monitoring your competition. Do not get lazy, but also do not emulate. Be authentic with your offerings and be sure you are providing something unique. Focus on innovation; this will help you maintain a strong brand and increase your chances of building customer loyalty.

Be authentic and unique.

3.7 BUILDING AND MAINTAINING MORALE

As a team leader, you must develop an understanding of the art of management and communication. No matter how good you are at your craft, if you are difficult to deal with, people will avoid you, and it will damage your personal brand. Focus on building healthy working relationships with all your stakeholders. This includes your executive team and your members. As discussed in Secret 1, focus on adding value. Let's look at some ways in which you can build and maintain morale in your student organization or business.

3.7.1 INSTILLING A SENSE OF OWNERSHIP

If you want quality results, you have to practice quality communication. Get to know your team. Let them know you appreciate them. Remind each person that he or she is a valued member of your team. This will help instill a sense of ownership in your student organization or company. People respond favorably to positive reinforcement in the form of feedback. When we know we have done something well, we feel good about it and want to repeat the performance, perhaps even enhance the performance in the future.

3.7.2 SHOWING APPRECIATION AND RESPECT

When you show appreciation, your team will appreciate you. This creates a welcoming working environment, and can positively influence your employees' performance. This can be done in the form of something as simple as an acknowledgement either publically or privately, for work done well. Think of ways you can show appreciation for your team members. Feelings of appreciation are linked to job satisfaction.[11]

3.7.3 BEING COMMUNICABLY WELCOMING

When delegating tasks, clearly communicate instructions and due dates to the person or people responsible for completing the task. Also, let them know you are available should they have any questions. Finally, be sure to follow up with them to see how the task is coming along. Touch points are very important. We are all very busy but usually people respond well to follow-ups. Something as simple as asking how the project is going should suffice. Treat your team members as individuals, not as subordinates.

---

11 The Effects of Employee Recognition and Appreciation. (n.d.). Retrieved April 20, 2016, from https://www.tinypulse.com.

3.7.4 PROVIDING GROWTH OPPORTUNITIES

When you provide new opportunities to your team members, it shows them you are interested in their development and success. This, in itself, helps improve morale because it shows your team you care about them and want them to succeed. Always be on the lookout for growth opportunities for your team members. Think of each person's skill set and how they may relate to potential future deliverables. For example, if your company has been invited to write a brief blog post about a certain topic related to your industry, and you have a receptionist that blogs on her spare time, ask her to be a part of this task. This may include editing the article, or even writing it entirely. The point is to invest in your team.

Secret 4

REGISTRATION

Once you have formed your leadership team and secured members, you will need to register your student organization with your college or university. This Secret is about the process of identifying and submitting the commonly required paperwork to do this. The majority of this Secret covers information on registering a business.

4.1 IDENTIFYING YOUR STUDENT AFFAIRS/ACTIVITIES CENTER

Many colleges and universities have a Student Affairs or Student Activities Center. This is typically where students can gather information on scholarship opportunities, academic events, and administrative tasks required to register campus clubs. Find this location on your college or university and inquire about the requirements associated with registering your student organization.

In many cases, you are required to draft and submit a Bylaws and Constitution for your student organization. In this capacity, it is in your best interest to involve your Board Advisor as well as your entire executive committee in the process of creating these documents.

4.1.1 SUBMITTING CHAPTER BYLAWS AND CONSTITUTION

Due to the complexities of these papers, they might be working documents for some predetermined amount of time. Try to create them as soon as possible, however, because they are typically pre-requisites to lifting restriction limitations such as the ability to reserve rooms, etc.[1] As soon as the documents are complete, submit them to your Student Affairs/Activities Office. If this is not the process for your institution, it is at least a good place to start. Investigate the process and plan accordingly. When creating your Bylaws and Constitution, each point should be clearly defined within the respective documents. Each document should state the dates of origination, and revisions when applicable.

4.1.2 PROCURING OTHER REQUIRED DOCUMENTATION

Other often-required materials include a request for such information as total number of current members and other things that pertain specifically to your organization. This information request may vary from one academic institution to another so be sure to inquire accordingly with your college or university.

4.1.3 AMENDING DOCUMENTATION

It may eventually become apparent that your organization documentation needs to be updated to reflect current operations. The directors and stakeholders can amend organizational documents. In the case of a student organization, the directors are those individuals holding leadership positions, and the stakeholders are the members of your organization, which includes the members of your leadership committee. This is typically done via a formal voting process but can be done informally as well depending on how you decide to run your organization. Make sure that whatever changes you make to your Bylaws, they are consistent with the regulations imposed and maintained by your college or university. If you have any specific questions about regulations, contact your Student Affairs/Activities Center.

---

1 Download the FREE templates at https://www.patrickgreenough.com/resources.

SUMMARY AND APPLICATIONS TO ENTREPRENEURSHIP

After you secure an executive team and member base, inquire with your academic institution about the paperwork required to register your student organization. While often-required documents include Bylaws and Constitution, other documents may also be necessary. Be sure to look into the requirements with your college or university and act accordingly. Decide on how you wish to implement the document emendation process and include this information into your Bylaws.

Just like registering a student organization, registering a business requires you to file a series of documents. The following instructions are provided to help you understand the administrative process for registering your business.

4.2 FILING THE DOCUMENTS REQUIRED TO START A BUSINESS

When you start a business, law requires you to file specific documents with the state in which you live. This includes procuring at least the following items in order:

1. Doing Business As (DBA) (a.k.a., Fictitious Business Name (FBN))
2. Adjudication
3. Business Bank Account
4. Employee Identification Number (EIN)

This section will explain how to register your business name with your county for legal and tax reporting purposes. This process includes: how to register a Doing Business As/Fictitious Business Name (DBA/FBN) with your county; adjudication; how to set up a business account with your bank; and how to secure an Employee Identification Number (EIN) with the Internal Revenue Service (IRS). The content in this section is meant to act as an instruction manual for completing this four-step process. All of these steps are necessary and often legally required when operating an income producing entity. This content is highly applicable to post-graduate entrepreneurial endeavors.

4.2.1 REGISTERING A "DOING BUSINESS AS" (DBA) / "FICTITIOUS BUSINESS NAME" (FBN)

If you have a viable organization or business that makes money, you need to track all income and report it to the IRS at the end of the year, preferably under your business name. To do that, secure a Doing Business As (DBA) a.k.a. Fictitious Business Name (FBN). Each county has a unique FBN registration process so be sure to investigate your county's filing requirements so that you can proceed accordingly. Filing online is more convenient, but it can come with a lengthy lead-time while the in-person option allows for same day registration.

If for some reason, you want to modify your existing FBN, you will need to access your account where the FBN was registered. In your account, you should have the option to access specific forms related to the FBN registration process. Select the correct form and proceed accordingly. If you cannot find the appropriate forms but would still like to modify your existing FBN, contact your FBN filing department for guidance.

If you set up an FBN in one county and move to another county to continue doing business, you should file a New FBN Statement with the county of your current residence and either let your previous FBN expire or file a New Abandonment Statement with the county of your previous residence.[2] You are responsible for making sure your FBN is available in your current county. If the name of the FBN you had in your previous county is not available in your current county, you will need to use a different name for your new FBN. When you register your new FBN, you will need to adjudicate and revise the name of your business bank account. Currently, when you update the FBN on file with the IRS, you can keep the same EIN that was associated with your previous FBN.

4.2.2 PROCESSING ADJUDICATION

Whenever you interact with the FBN process, i.e., register, revise, abandon, withdrawal, etc., you may be required to publish this action in a local newspaper

---

2 FBN expiration is a cost savings since it costs you nothing to let it expire.

within 30 days of filing. This process is called adjudication. Request a list of adjudicated newspapers in the area associated with the Registrar/Clerk-Recorder where you filed. You will likely be informed about this process when you register your initial FBN but if you are not, be sure to inquire about it.

4.2.3 SETTING UP A BUSINESS BANK ACCOUNT

Once registered, the Registrar/Clerk-Recorder will provide you with a certified copy of your DBA/FBN. Your bank will need to see this in order to create your business account. The name of your business account will be the same name as your DBA/FBN. The process for arranging this with your bank should include a sit-down meeting with a business banker.

When you set up your business account, you will likely be required to manage two separate associated accounts: Savings and Checking. Each account will require some minimal amount of funds to keep it operational. To prevent monthly fees, you may also be required to transfer funds into one of the accounts each month. If your company is still in the monetization development phase, you may not be in a strong enough financial position to add money to your accounts right out of the gate. Here is a trick to making transfers each month without actually adding any money to your business bank account. Set up automatic transfers to take place each month on two consecutive days.[3] Let's look at an example of this monthly money shuffle.

* **Transfer 1:** The 15th of every month. Auto transfer $100 from Checking to Savings
* **Transfer 2:** The 16th of every month. Auto transfer $100 from Savings to Checking

Most banks provide their customers with online banking, which allows you to easily create automatic transfer arrangements from your account portal. If your bank does not yet offer online banking, request this service to be set up. This will prevent you from paying monthly fees associated with

---

3 Discuss this with a business banker to ensure acceptability.

maintaining a business bank account. Additionally, automatic transfers will prevent you from forgetting to implement a manual transfer, which will prevent missed transfer fees should they exist. The only disadvantage is that the $200 ($100 in each account - Checking and Savings) is locked in your Business Bank Account.

One of the primary benefits of creating a business account with your bank is it separates the distribution flow of your personal and business funds. This is highly desirable for any legal action. Additionally, it will help you keep track of income for tax reporting to the IRS at the end of the year.

Once your business account is set up, you may be issued a debit card and pin number. No matter how much money your business makes, make sure to use the debit card at least once a year to prevent it from becoming inactive. If you do not use it, some banks may charge you a monthly fee after one year of inactivity. If that happens, notify your bank. Some banks may issue you a new debit card and pin number and remind you of this process so that you can prevent this going forward.

4.2.4 SECURING AN EMPLOYEE IDENTIFICATION NUMBER (EIN)

An Employee Identification Number (EIN) is used to identify a business entity.[4] Securing an EIN is the fourth and final step in the process of registering your business with your county. The EIN is 9 digits and is usually written as 00-0000000. You use this number when you report your income to the Internal Revenue Service (IRS) for tax purposes. You are legally required to report accurate information so make sure to tally all your income. Some helpful options for recording income are Microsoft Excel, and Google Sheets.[5] If an accountant files your taxes for you, they will appreciate reviewing this document, as it will help reduce the lead-time to procuring your tax returns. To retrieve your EIN, contact the IRS directly.[6] You may be required to file Form SS-4 so make sure to inquire about both the EIN and SS-4 with the IRS.

---

4 Employer ID Numbers. (n.d.). Retrieved April 20, 2016, from http://www.irs.gov.

5 Greenough, P. D. (2015, July 25). How to Convert an Excel File into a Google Sheet. Retrieved April 20, 2016, from https://www.patrickgreenough.com.

6 Contact Your Local IRS Office. (n.d.). Retrieved April 20, 2016, from https://www.irs.gov.

4.3 REPORTING EARNINGS

Once you have registered your business, track the flow of money into and out of your business. Tracking cost and revenue will allow you to properly report your annual earning to the IRS.

Your taxable earned income is your net earnings if you are self-employed and own or operate a business. The IRS requires that you report your earnings if you make over a certain amount annually.[7] Errors may result in costly fines and penalties. It is in your best interest to accurately report your financial information. Think critically, act logically, and whatever you do, be honest.

> Think critically, act logically, and whatever you do, be honest.

4.3.1 PREPARING TAXES

Your taxes can be prepared and submitted by you, your accountant, or a third party. If you live in a metropolis, your city will likely have several local tax preparation vendors from which to choose. The forms required to file your taxes are dependent upon the type of business entity you have. In the next section, we will discuss the different types of business structures. Make sure to talk to your tax preparer ahead of time about which forms you need to file.

4.4 CREATING AN INCORPORATION (INC.)

Incorporation declares the business as a corporate entity and will protect the owner from company liabilities. If you have multiple income producing entities, you should consider incorporating each one to protect them from each other should legal trouble occur for any single one of your incorporated businesses. Each state has a unique licensing process so be sure to investigate the process in your area.

---

7 Self-Employed Individuals Tax Center. (n.d.). Retrieved April 20, 2016, from http://www.irs.gov.

4.5 UNDERSTANDING THE TYPES OF BUSINESS STRUCTURES

When you start a business, you need to decide on the proper structure of business entity to establish. Different structures require different tax forms. The IRS lists the following types of business structures:[8]

4.5.1 SOLE PROPRIETORSHIP:

You are unincorporated, and you own the business by yourself.

4.5.2 PARTNERSHIPS:

You and at least one other person own the business together

4.5.3 CORPORATIONS:

Your firm allows prospective shareholders to exchange property and/or money for capital stock.

4.5.4 S CORPORATIONS:

Your firm passes profits and losses through your personal income tax, which allows you, as the owner, to avoid double taxation. Also known as a Small Business Corporation.

4.5.5 LIMITED LIABILITY COMPANY (LLC):

Depending on the jurisdictions in your state, you, as the owner, are provided with protection from personal liability.

---

8 Business Structures. (n.d.). Retrieved April 20, 2016, from http://www.irs.gov.

4.6 UNDERSTANDING STRUCTURES FOR MULTIPLE BUSINESSES

If you operate more than one business, each business should be set up uniquely and financially separate. For example, say you have two businesses, and you want to set up a structure for them, i.e., Sole Proprietorship; Partnership; Corporation; S Corporation; Limited Liability Company (LLC), each business should be set up with its own structure. This will protect you and the other businesses in the event of legal action.[9]

4.7 CLOSING A BUSINESS ENTITY

Businesses close for many reasons. Some common causes are poor strategic planning, undesirable product or service offerings, niche market not sustainably significant, inadequate market locations, etc. Should you decide to close your business entity, you will need to complete the necessary steps.[10] The process typically involves filing any outstanding tax returns and balances and submitting the proper closing forms with your Secretary of State (SOS). It is likely that the refined details vary by state so investigate the process requirements in your area.

Closing a business entity in any form does not revoke the legal status of its tax requirements or liabilities. For example, any outstanding taxes must be paid along with any associated pending deliverables. It is critical to be aware of your personal responsibilities as they relate to your business. Get more information about this by contacting your state's Franchise Tax Board.

---

9 This is especially applicable in the real estate industry. It's common practice for agents to create unique LLCs for each of their income properties.

10 Closing a Business. (n.d.). Retrieved April 20, 2016, from http://www.irs.gov.

Secret 5

PROGRAMMING

This Secret focuses specifically on how to plan your roster of events for the coming year, and how to have your first meeting. We will cover the planning process, meeting times, and meeting collateral materials. Your student organization should always strive for a low or no-cost strategy regarding programming. Keep this in mind when reading this Secret and think about ways in which your organization can keep spending requirements low while providing total programming value.[1] Avoid sacrificing quality for savings. Be sure to invest in your brand where necessary to ensure quality maintenance. Be frugal without being cheap.

> Be frugal without being cheap.

Whenever and wherever you have an event, it is important to announce the names of the board members in attendance and ask them to identify themselves. This helps build awareness of the executive board and provides attendees with an understanding of who to contact if they are interested in contributing skills under an area managed by a respective board member. For

---

1 For new organizations, track all incurred expenses for year one to create a benchmark for year two.

example, if I were interested in planning events, I would find it beneficial to identify the VP Programming so that we can connect and converse about event planning.

5.1 PLANNING

Ideally, you will want to plan your entire year before you have your first member meeting. This is important for generating credibility for your organization, and allowing members the chance to look forward to specific events and plan accordingly. Before your first meeting, you should schedule meaningful, relevant, educational, and professionally enriching activities. Some suggestions are as follows:

* Inter-Organizational Group Collaborations
* Volunteer Activities
* Workshops
* Networking Events

Take some time to plan out your year.[2] The longer you have to plan, the better and more efficient the planning process will become. If you are a sole operator, you will have to do all of the planning yourself. The advantage is you have complete control over how to plan your year. As the year progresses and you secure an executive team, you can delegate responsibilities accordingly. Let's specifically discuss each of the planning activities as indicated in the above bullet points.

5.1.1 CREATING INTER-ORGANIZATIONAL GROUP COLLABORATIONS

Group cohesion is a strategic way to strengthen awareness of your organization. When your student organization collaborates with another student

---

2 This can be done the summer before the fall semester that hosts the first meeting. If it's late fall and your leadership tenure begins in the spring, plan as you go but start as soon as possible.

organization, both organizations can benefit greatly. Here are some of the ways both parties can benefit:

5.1.1.1 Building New and Strengthening Existing Relationships

When you build relationships with other organizations, it improves morale, creates sharing opportunities, allows your members to interact with others, simplifies common logistical complexities, and provides for a more robust service offering to all involved stakeholders. These connections typically allow for knowledge sharing. If yours is a new student organization, you may not be aware of the many processes required to optimally run your organization, or how to implement them. When you interact with others who have some experience doing these things, you can learn from them.

Usually, when you plan a jointly sponsored event, both organizations benefit. It is often very easy to gain process knowledge just from the event planning process alone. Process knowledge involves everything from how to reserve rooms, to understanding trade partnership deliverables, to optimal marketing strategies. Finally, both organizations may have different event concept ideas. The sharing of these ideas will enable both organizations to become more creative and service oriented. When this occurs, your offerings will become more salient.

You may not be able to make room reservations until your organization has submitted the proper registration forms to your Student Affairs/Activities Office and they have been approved.[3] If your registration paperwork is pending, but you would still like to reserve a room for a meeting, get a registered and relevant organization to sponsor the event and ask them to reserve the room for the meeting. This is a helpful workaround until the proper forms have been submitted to and approved by your academic institution.

5.1.1.2 Strengthening Brand Awareness

Brand awareness is integral to the success of your student organization. When you capture partnerships with existing accommodating and/or competing

---

3 Bylaws and Constitution are covered in section 4.1.1.

organizations, it sends a message to your target audience that your organization is collaborative and dynamic. Both of these characteristics will positively contribute to your growing brand. Additionally, forming new partnerships enhances the probability of securing additional progressive opportunities. People talk, so when you contribute positively to something in someone's life, you have a higher likelihood of being considered when something comes along that is related to your skill set.

This is a lot like the discussion about finding new clients in section 1.2.1. When you work with others, you build trust. When trust is built, you have a higher likelihood of being considered for additional opportunities when they come along. It is the same with student organizational partnering. If the partnering organization is developing a new idea for an event and needs some help on initiatives that require skills they know your organization possesses, they are much more likely to call on your organization, which will lead to the further development of your organization's brand.

5.1.1.3 *Utilizing Cross-Audience Marketing*

Collaborating with other organizations allows for consolidated marketing efforts. This occurs in the form of marketing the partnered event to the target audiences of both student organizations. For example, if your organization has an audience of 500 and the partnering organization has an audience of 500, you have a total yield of 1000 potential event attendees. This will significantly increase the chances of increasing your attendee number averages at your events, which is always the goal. While most events hosted by student organizations are offered at no charge to students, for paid events, more attendees equate to more money.[4]

5.1.2 UNDERSTANDING VOLUNTEER ACTIVITIES

Temporarily donating your time to a worthwhile cause is a great way to improve the humanitarian element of your brand. It is also very charitable

---

4 While you might never charge students to attend your events, this is something to consider when or if you decide to plan a professional event outside of academia.

and shows the community that your student organization cares. While civic activities may not directly relate to your organization's service offerings, they are valuable character-building opportunities. In this section, we will discuss some of the possible types of volunteer activities you may consider when planning your year. If you can successfully secure and carry out any of these opportunities, take the time to build relationships with the vendors involved. Then parlay that into potentially securing volunteer days with these vendors on a quarterly basis. This will simplify the planning process for future quarters. Keep track of contact information in an Excel or Google Sheet for easy accessibility for future planning initiatives.[5]

5.1.2.1 Soup Kitchens and/or Food Banks

Look for these areas in your city. If you live in a metropolitan area, the chances are high that your city has a soup kitchen or food bank, or something like it. If you find one, make contact and inquire about the possibility of arranging a day and time for your organization to assist in service activities.

5.1.2.2 City Cleanup

These activities include anything pertaining to cleaning an area of your city. If you live by the ocean, you might contact your city to secure a day and time to pick up trash around the shoreline. If you live inland, see if you can secure a day and time to clean up a road median or other area in your town. You can also inquire about other areas that need to be cleaned.

5.1.2.3 Campus Volunteering

Volunteering your time to give back to your campus in some way can help develop, strengthen, and maintain the reputation of your student organization. Campus volunteer activities come in a variety of forms; it just depends on what is happening on your campus at the time. Some universities decorate

---

5 Google Drive is covered in section 6.3.4.

their campus around the holidays. Depending on the size of your campus and the intended level of decoration, those involved may appreciate the extra help. Take advantage of this opportunity to volunteer your organization to provide the extra help. Other campus volunteer activities may include: assisting in setting up program initiatives for Freshman Orientation; setting up chairs and tables at graduation ceremonies; and hosting campus tours to prospective students.

If you want to be more progressive, you can offer tutoring services to the campus community based on the skill sets of your members. For example, if your organization involves mathematics, you might create an arrangement where your members can assist math students with homework questions. If your organization is more about business, you might create an opportunity for your members to provide advice to entrepreneurial students. These are just some examples of campus volunteer activities.

5.1.3 UNDERSTANDING WORKSHOPS

Another way to offer value is to arrange workshops that provide education. Aim to provide education relevant to your target audience. Continuing with the previous examples, if your organization is based in mathematics, provide workshops on something related to math. If your organization is based in business, provide workshops related to business. The key is to generate content relevant to your target audience. The following is a list of examples of events that would fall into this category.

5.1.3.1 *Panel Discussions*

A panel occurs when a small group of individuals is brought together to discuss and investigate content and questions related to a specific topic. Secure key people for your Panel who have expertise in the particular fields of study related to the topic area covered in your panel discussion. For example, if your panel will discuss corporate social responsibility, secure panelists with executive titles or extensive experience in the fields of green marketing, ethics, and recycling. Identify panelists who can contribute to meaningful dialogue in the specific area of interest.

The structure of a panel usually occurs when the panelists sit at a table or series of tables and answer questions posed by a moderator. The audience listens to the dialogue and is sometimes provided with opportunities to ask the panelists questions. This arrangement can be very educational, and audience members may gain valuable insights learned from seasoned professionals. This is just one example, and arrangements may vary depending on your preference.

5.1.3.2 Guest Speakers

Another great way to add value to your members is to provide them with valuable networking opportunities with local professionals. Getting face time with key local executives in fields relevant to your student organization can sometimes be difficult, so these interactions are highly desirable. One of the main advantages of interacting with high-level professionals is the strong potential for finding internships, full or part-time work, contractual work (1099), or even consulting. Audience members are encouraged to bring business cards and dress appropriately when interacting with high-level professionals.[6]

An optimal way to secure guest speakers for your events is very similar to the way in which you would request permission from instructors or professors to pitch to their classes. As discussed in section 3.1.3, your invitation should be made up of two parts: Acknowledgement and Request. Aim to secure speakers that are practicing in the profession most desired by your member base. For example, if many of your members are majoring in marketing, secure marketing executives as guest speakers. Try to match the professions of your guest speakers to the primary fields of study of your target audience. This will add the most value to these events.

Finding guest speakers can be done in a variety of ways. Start by reviewing your social network via email Rolodex, and LinkedIn. Direct connections make these invitations easier. If one of your contacts is connected to someone you do not know but would like to invite to be a guest speaker, request an introduction from the shared connection. You can request an introduction via email or LinkedIn.

---

6 For a review of networking etiquette, refer to Secret 1.

5.1.4 UNDERSTANDING NETWORKING EVENTS

One of the primary benefits of being part of a student organization is capitalizing on robust networking opportunities. This is often the main reason why people join organizations; they want to enhance their networks. In business, your goal is to solve a problem. In this case, it is to give people what they want. If your audience members want to build their networks, make it a point to incorporate networking opportunities into each event within your event roster. All of the event types listed in this Secret are great networking opportunities.

5.2 MEETING TIMES AND COLLATERAL MATERIALS

Once you have planned your roster of events for the coming year, you are ready to schedule your first meeting of the academic calendar term or semester. Be sure to have copies of your annual calendar available to hand out to attendees at the conclusion of the meeting. Wait until the meeting has ended before handing out the calendar. It is important to have your audience's full attention throughout the duration of the first meeting. If you provide handouts early, attention will be drawn away from you and toward the content on the handout. It is best not to mention the handout until you provide it at the end of the meeting. In the meantime, discuss the roster of events as an action item on the meeting agenda. This strategy will help capture attention, and increase engagement.

Once you have the meeting structure planned, you need to decide what time during the day to have it. The character of student organizations will vary depending on the school, the leadership, and the makeup of the student body. All of these factors influence the decision regarding when to have your first meeting. If you plan to have an evening meeting, secure food for attendees so they can concentrate on your message and not their hunger.[7] Additionally, offering food is a gracious incentive to attend the meeting. This will make attendees happy, and make your organization look favorable. If you are having your first meeting during the day, plan to provide some refreshments then

---

7 This is ideal if your event takes place around dinnertime.

as well.[8] It is up to you but consider food and how it relates to the timing of your meeting.

A strategic approach to accommodate the food situation for your event is to invite a local restaurant or deli to sponsor it. The trade partnership might look like this: the sponsor provides food for the event, and in return your organization includes the sponsor's logo and/or a mention of the sponsor in all of your marketing materials and social media schedules for the event. This is a great way to build partnerships and secure food for your events at minimal monetary cost if any at all. To reiterate the key point in the introduction of this Secret, the focus is to strive for a low or no-cost strategy.

8 Common options include veggie trays and bottled water or pizza and soft drinks.

SECRET 5: PROGRAMMING

SUMMARY AND APPLICATIONS TO ENTREPRENEURSHIP

When planning your roster of events for the year, consider the "How" and "What" of event planning. Work with your team to discuss the potential for planning any one of the following types of events: inter-organizational group collaborations; volunteer activities; workshops; and networking events. After you have confirmed an event schedule, secure a date and venue for your first members' meeting. It is important to provide a schedule of events to your attendees, but it is strongly encouraged to wait until the meeting concludes before handing it out. Consider the time of day your meeting will take place. Plan to provide food as a welcome.

For the remainder of this Secret, we will discuss programming with an emphasis on monetization from a professional, or business standpoint. This Secret will conclude with a conversation on the benefits of strategic alliances, as well as how to identify them. These concepts are meant to facilitate your mastery of the subject area as well as help you think of how strategic alliances pertain to your business objectives.

5.3 UNDERSTANDING CONFERENCES

There are two ways to go about adding a conference into your event roster: implementing one yourself, or co-sponsoring one with another entity. Conference planning is extensive and takes time. A common lead-time for conference planning is 6-8 months. To get a feel for this process, try co-sponsoring a conference with someone else first before tackling the implementation process on your own. Let's discuss both options in more detail.

5.3.1 IMPLEMENTATION

If your business is planning to implement a conference, follow these steps in order:

1. Secure a date
2. Secure a venue

3. Recruit a Planning Committee or Advisory Board
   - The Planning Committee or Advisory Board is the team that will be meeting regularly either in person or on conference calls to work through the planning process. This team is made up of the executive leadership of your organization, and anyone else you feel could effectively help in the planning process. It is typically encouraged to select high profile seasoned professionals within the field of study that themes the event. For example, if you are implementing a marketing conference, scout people who possess executive titles and/or experience in the field of marketing.
4. Identify a conference theme
5. Secure an event schedule
   - This pertains to event structure, which might include any or all of the following: panel discussions; round tables; keynote speakers, etc.
   - Identify what events will happen when and where they will occur throughout the day.
6. Initiate a marketing campaign
7. Secure guest speakers
8. Secure an Audio/Visual (AV) Technician
   - Secure an AV Technician if your speakers will be giving presentations, or if you plan on recording the event.
9. Determine a food menu and associated vendor(s) where applicable
10. Arrange for parking
11. Create, deploy, and analyze a post-event attendee survey
    - This will give you clearer indications of attendee satisfaction, which will help you refine the conference in the future.
    - Survey software suggestions: SurveyMonkey, and Google Forms
12. Plan a post-event debriefing meeting with your Planning Committee or Advisory Board. Action items to cover during the debrief meeting:
    - Event revenue and net profit
    - Total number of attendees

o General thoughts on specific segments of the event: panel discussions; round tables; keynote speakers, etc.

o Overview of the completed attendee surveys

5.3.2 SPONSORSHIP

If you are new to the conference planning process, you might consider being a sponsor. Sponsorship requires a significantly reduced time commitment in comparison to its implementation counterpart. Sponsoring an event is wise if your business is planning a series of other events throughout the year. The planning process can be complex and if your business is planning several events in a single year, enlisting help from other businesses can create process flow efficiencies in the planning process. Aim to align your available bandwidth with the aggregated planning process for the year's roster of events. Be realistic about your forecast and always allow for at least a modest cushion. Do not be afraid to ask for help.

When sponsoring an event, the arrangement can be monetary, trade, or some combination of both that makes up a tailored customized arrangement. Let's discuss each.

5.3.2.1 *Monetary Sponsorship:*

Monetary Sponsorship occurs when your business provides a predetermined sum of money to the implementing party, and in return, your business receives corresponding benefits based on the amount of funds provided. If the party implementing the conference is offering sponsorship benefits, there may be a possibility that a tier structure exists. Here is an example of such a structure:

* **Gold Level:** $10,000. Benefits include your logo at the top (header) of the sponsorship page on their website, 30 social mentions, and 6 complimentary enrollments.
* **Silver Level:** $5,000. Benefits include your logo in the middle of the sponsorship page on their website, 20 social mentions, and 4 complimentary enrollments.

    *   **Bronze Level:** $2,500. Benefits include your logo at the bottom (footer) of the sponsorship page on their website, 10 social mentions, and 2 complimentary enrollments.

5.3.2.2 Trade Sponsorship:

Trade Sponsorship occurs when your business provides benefits in return for other benefits provided by the party implementing the event. For example, you could offer coverage of the conference on your website in the form of a blog post written by a member of the implementing party. You might also include a web advertisement for the conference on your website in return for social mentions and complimentary enrollments to the conference. These are just some examples. Ensure both parties are clear about the responsibilities pertaining to their side of the trade agreement.

5.3.2.3 Tailored Customized Sponsorship:

A more involved approach is Tailored Customized Sponsorship.[9] This type of sponsorship agreement requires both parties to discuss what specifically they wish to gain from the partnership. If your organization is requesting the sponsorship, ask the prospective sponsor how they wish to be involved in the event, then create an agreement that accommodates their level of commitment. Create a price that matches the perceived ROI[10] of the agreement. For example, if the sponsoring party wants to supply the keynote speaker, but wants to be left out of the planning process entirely, note this when creating a price point for that sponsor. Do not be shy here; this is where you have negotiation power. The following are some examples of such arrangements where you can match price points

---

9 "Dialogue with Andrew Cortez, 2013-2014 VP of Sponsorship for San Diego AMA During the Spring 2014 Regional Retreat for the American Marketing Association," Conversation with Patrick Greenough.

10 Return on Investment (ROI) is a process used to measure and compare an investments return with its associated cost.

with sponsor involvement expectations.[11] Plan to couple price points should the sponsor want a complete package or some variation of different opportunities.

* **$10,000.** Sponsor requests to provide the keynote speaker
* **$5,000.** Sponsor requests to host a panel
* **$2,500.** Sponsor requests to set up a promotion table

5.4 DEVELOPING STRATEGIC PARTNERSHIPS

Strategic alliances can be very beneficial to businesses that want to expand into new markets. New market expansion allows you to grow and capture new audiences, which builds your brand. When scouting strategic partnerships, it is important to identify opportunities that are mutually beneficial to both parties. This includes finding businesses that, with your core competencies, allow you and them to cater to new markets.

Partnerships exist in all facets of industry, and they allow companies to increase brand awareness and reach new markets. Here are two examples of notable partnerships that have resulted in success for the companies involved.

eBay and PayPal: PayPal offers a streamlined approach to making payments, and it makes a profit on each transaction made on eBay, one of the world's leading auction websites.

Taco Bell and Doritos: In Spring 2012, Taco Bell released the Doritos Locos Taco (DLT). This project was an initiative that resulted from a partnership between Taco Bell, and Doritos. Through this partnership, Taco Bell created new technology to form the Doritos-inspired shell of a Taco Bell taco.[12] Just over a year after inception, Taco Bell had recorded sales of over 500 million DLTs.[13]

---

11 These prices are more commonly found in sponsorship agreements for professional organizations. These numbers will likely be drastically lower for most student organizations that offer similar packages.

12 Carr, A. (2013, May 1). Deep Inside Taco Bell's Doritos Locos Taco. Retrieved April 20, 2016, from http://www.fastcompany.com.

13 Ayrouth, E. (2013, May 16). BREAKING: Taco Bell Has Now Sold Over Half a Billion Doritos Locos Tacos. Retrieved April 20, 2016, from http://www.foodbeast.com.

When investigating alliance opportunities, think of what you can do to benefit the partnership. In approaching a potential alliance partner, it is important to focus less on how the partnership can benefit you and more on how you can benefit the partnership. This is consistent with the methodologies we discussed about offering instead of asking for value in section 1.2.7. The same applies to identifying partnerships. Once you do this, you will be more aligned with your core goal, which is to attract and maintain mutually profitable strategic partnerships.

5.4.1 BENEFITING FROM STRATEGIC PARTNERSHIPS

Creating strategic partnerships comes with benefits. Some are listed here:

5.4.1.1 Market Reach Augmentation

When you partner with another organization, both organizations benefit by enhancing market reach. Each firm will market to its respective list. For example, firm A markets the joint event to its list, and firm B markets the joint event to its list. If firm A has an audience of 500 and it is partnering with firm B that also has an audience of 500, then the combined possible market reach would be 1000.

5.4.1.2 Minimizing Risk and Maximizing Efficiency

Risk is inevitable with all interactions and processes. How it is managed is what makes the difference. Regarding partnerships, consider that process complexities increase with the addition of more people. Communication needs to be clearly and carefully implemented to ensure that objectives are carried out by the agreed upon parties. When this is not the case, it can create confusion, diminish communication quality, hurt the brand for both organizations, and compromise the partnership. Let's look at an example and how to avoid such pitfalls.

For this example, we will use the same firms we discussed who have a total combined audience of 1000. Both firms are located in the same town and share relationships with a variety of contacts in the area. Firm A and firm

B both offer services in the same category of Lead Generation. Together, they want to host a one-day seminar on Lead Generation, so they begin scouting and building relationships with local venues. To ensure an efficient process and to minimize confusion, each firm should agree to a unique set of responsibilities regarding venue procurement and reservation. One firm might scout actual locations while the other might research catering options. There is no reason for both firms to be managing both things at the same time; it is inefficient and can quickly create confusion. For optimal process control, each firm should manage a unique set of relationships and responsibilities. Contact management is an integral piece of partnership acquisition and event planning. You want to make it easy for both parties to work well with one another.

5.4.1.3 *Brainstorming*

In the field of Project Management, the ridiculous phrase "throw more bodies at it" was once commonly used to refer to adding additional resources to a project in an attempt to fix a problem or accommodate work-in-process (WIP). Here, we agree but instead of more bodies and problems, we are using more brains to think of different ways to collaborate and add value to the target audience. While this may be intuitive to some, it may be overlooked by organizations with old-fashioned or authoritarian working styles. The more people you have, the more ideas you are likely to have. Be sure to encourage open communication with your internal stakeholders, as it will help build confidence and enhance group cohesion and morale, which will work in everyone's favor.

Secret 6

STRATEGIC PLANNING

For this Secret, we will discuss how to implement the strategic planning process known as the World Café, and what to cover during an Officer Retreat for your student organization.

6.1 IMPLEMENTING THE WORLD CAFÉ

The World Café is a conversational activity designed to provide deeper insights into the various elements of organizational processes.[1] It is an easy and effective format for hosting large group dialogue.[2] Those involved in this activity include all primary stakeholders directly affected by the progress of the organization. This may include but is not limited to the executive leaders, general members, and anyone else that contributes to the organization at the executive level. For student organizations, this may also include faculty and staff. To implement this exercise, follow these detailed instructions in the order listed.

---

1 My first exposure to the World Café was with the national executive board and affiliate leadership of the National Human Resources Association (NHRA) at an annual leadership retreat in Plantation, FL in September 2013.

2 World Café Method. (n.d.). Retrieved April 20, 2016, from http://www.theworldcafe.com.

6.1.1 DESIGNING THE QUESTION SET

During this phase, create a list of questions each related to a specific area and pertaining to the growth of the organization. These questions may include reference to membership growth, revenue generation, website development, etc. The idea is to create open-ended questions that will generate discussions with a high probability of offering insights not garnered in traditional peer-to-peer conversation. Let's look at some examples of questions.

* With regard to our website, what are some changes you would like to see implemented to enhance user experience?
* What are some strategies that we can implement to grow our membership numbers during the current fiscal year?
* How can we increase our revenue and net profit, and how/where should we be spending our funds?
* What are some ways we can partner with other organizations?

6.1.2 FORMING TEAMS: THE 1-2-3-4 METHOD

Once you have identified a list of questions, form as many teams as there are questions. For example, if you have four questions, create four teams. Go around the room and ask each person to count off, the next person will say the next number in order. For example, the first person says one; the second person says two, and so on. If you have four questions, stop and restart your numbers at four. Once everyone in the room has counted off, ask them to form groups corresponding to their respective numbers. All of the One's form a group, all of the Two's form a group, etc. all the way up to the last number as indicated by the number of questions. Each group should have its own table and group moderator.

6.1.3 MODERATING THE GROUP

One person at each table is given one of the four questions. This person will be the moderator and recorder of all key points from the discussions surrounding his or her specific question. The moderator should record discussion feedback by way of pen and paper, or computer.[3]

Each group is given 15 minutes to discuss answers to their question. After 15 minutes has passed, the moderator stays at his or her table with the same question, but the group migrates to another table to discuss answers to another question posed at that table with the corresponding moderator. If there are four groups, this migration will occur four times. The moderators will record the feedback from all groups as they rotate through. This strategy will help better develop insights into answers to the four questions.

6.1.4 CURATING ANSWERS

Once all groups have had a chance to discuss answers to the questions posed, the moderators of each group will organize all the answers into categories based on the specific content areas associated with each question. For example, a question about the website will fall into the 'Website' category. A question about membership will fall into the 'Membership' category, etc. Each list should be written on a separate large piece of paper and hung on the wall(s) in the meeting room.

6.1.5 SELECTING ANSWERS BY SECTION

This is the final phase of the workshop. After all the answers are listed on sheets based on the respective categories, and posted on the wall(s) for all to see, request everyone in the room to get a pen and select only three items per category they feel are the most important. This process should be as simple as placing a checkmark next to an item.[4] Once everyone has made their selections, the majority ruling of where to place resources will be clearly revealed.

The point of the World Café is to reveal the most important areas of opportunity based on majority. It is a very simple process but provides extremely valuable insights. This process is highly recommended for any

---

3 Some program options include: Microsoft Word; TextEdit (Mac); and Notepad (PC).

4 Member responses may be affected by perceived political pressures should they exist.

team interested in gaining a deeper understanding of where to apply its resources.

6.2 PLANNING AN EXECUTIVE LEADERSHIP RETREAT

The Executive Retreat is a full-day strategy session, typically done annually, where the entire leadership team meets to discuss high-level topics related to the organization. This meeting is usually held at a secluded place on a weekend day, preferably on a Saturday. Try to locate a meeting space that has minimal distractions. Libraries, church buildings, and conference rooms are all possible venues for your Executive Retreat. Find one that is centrally located to all board members and reserve it at least one month in advance, or as early as possible.

The Executive Retreat is meant to cover executive level topics related to overall strategy for the organization. Regular updates should be reviewed during your leadership committee meetings throughout the year, which may be once or twice a month at most. The Executive Retreat should cover more high-level content. Follow the guidelines here for a review of who should attend and a list of potential topics to cover during your retreat.

Attendees. The following individuals should attend the Executive Retreat:

* All current board members
* Current board advisor if one exists. This could be a past board member, an executive staff member, or a professor. If they are actively involved in the growth of the Chapter, they should be in attendance.

Content. The following list of topics should be considered for discussion:

6.2.1 DEVELOPING YOUR CONSTITUTION AND BYLAWS

This is a great time to carve out the details for both of these documents.[5]

---

5 Bylaws and Constitution are covered in section 4.1.1.

6.2.2 DEVELOPING YOUR VISION, MISSION, VALUES, AND OBJECTIVES

* **Vision:** This is a statement that indicates the level and type of value your organization is currently offering.
* **Mission:** This is a statement that indicates the level and type of value your organization is constantly aiming to achieve.
* **Values:** This statement reflects the professional desires of your organization. This might include what your organization offers to its target audience.
* **Objectives:** This is a running list of what your organization hopes to achieve either on an ongoing basis or by some predetermined time.

6.2.3 DEVELOPING YOUR SWOT ANALYSIS

Identify the Strengths, Weaknesses, Opportunities, and Threats associated with your student organization.[6]

6.2.4 DEFINING OVERALL ORGANIZATIONAL GOALS FOR THE PROCEEDING YEAR

This may include a breakdown of goals for each officer in addition to that of the organization as a whole. Each board member should draft a list of 5-10 manageable goals to work toward in the coming year. Each goal should include a brief description and a strategy for how to obtain the goal. These lists should be submitted to the President for curation and total review.

6.2.5 DEFINING OFFICER ROLES

Roles must be clearly defined to allow for a smooth transition for new officers. It is important to be very specific about each role and understand that tasks should be delegated accordingly.[7]

---

6 SWOT Analysis is covered in section 3.6.

7 For examples of common officer roles, refer to section 2.2.

6.3 IMPLEMENTING SUCCESSION PLANNING STRATEGIES

6.3.1 UNDERSTANDING ELECTION TYPES

The following is a list of different types of elections and strategies to use to implement your succession plan.

6.3.1.1 *General Elections*

The general election process is designed for complete officer roster turnover. If you decide to allow only volunteers to run for office, you might consider the following strategy to implement the general election process:

1. Position the official election as its own event.
2. Have an election at the end of some predetermined amount of time, i.e., semester, or year.
3. The volunteers interested in running for office are given a chance to present their cases to the audience at the event.
4. After all the cases have been pitched for a particular position, each member of the audience is then encouraged to vote for a candidate. For a more streamlined approach to the voting process, you might use SurveyMonkey or Google Forms. Inviting audience members to write the name of their preferred candidate on a piece of paper to be collected is more primitive but just as effective.
5. Once all groups of votes have been collected, tally and select the new officers based on majority votes.

6.3.1.2 *Special Elections*

The special election process is designed for individual officer turnover. This might occur if an officer graduates, moves, or otherwise leaves his or her position prematurely. If this happens, consider implementing the following strategy:

1. The departing officer interviews a series of hand-selected volunteers to be considered as possible candidates to fill the position.

2. The departing officer then selects the optimal candidate and submits the recommendation to the remaining officers for review and feedback.
3. Once a candidate is selected, they are notified via email and introduced at the next chapter meeting.
4. Any candidates not selected for the position should be notified via email. The message should indicate sincere gratitude for their involvement and encouragement to stay involved and continue to develop their already impressive skill set. The key is to let them know that although they were not selected, their involvement is highly admired and greatly appreciated.

6.3.1.3 Responding to Opposition

This section describes how to position a verbal response to opposition from volunteers who were not selected to fill officer positions. If it does happen it will likely occur as a result of the special election process. The best way to handle this is to do the following:

1. Remain calm and collected.
2. Try to maintain a welcoming demeanor.
3. Let the party know that although they were not selected for an officer role, you admire his or her talent and look forward to watching them further develop their skills.
4. Listen and answer questions politely and with warm authenticity.

6.3.2 UNDERSTANDING ELECTION METHODS

However your organization decides to go about implementing the election process, your methods should be written into your Constitution. Consider the following strategies.

6.3.2.1 Who Should Run for Office

While not required, it is best to encourage volunteers to run for office. You already have rapport with them, and you are aware of their skill sets. Or, you can host open elections and let anyone run for office. The disadvantage to an open ballot is that you may possess limited knowledge of each candidate's abilities. Hopefully, each candidate's abilities will be advantageous to the organization, however, if you have not worked with someone previously, it is harder to gauge their likely impact on your organization. To overcome this hurdle, you might consider maintaining a list of prerequisites for interested candidates. This could include providing a letter or recommendation and/or a list of references. Try to create an opportunity for positive growth based on a best educated guess.

6.3.2.2 Election Frequency

Elections should be held at least once a year. While they may be held more frequently, it can make it harder to gain momentum on yearly goals. It is encouraged to run your elections once a year and preferably in December if the fiscal year starts on July 1st.

Investigate the fiscal year dates of your college or university and plan accordingly. If your fiscal year terms begin and end on July 1st of each year, plan to have elections in December. When this happens, official roles and responsibilities will not be activated until July 1st. The six months between December and July 1st should be used to train the elects.

6.3.2.3 Officer Elect Training

Officer Elect training should be a very robust learning experience for both the current and newly elected officer. The training process allows for knowledge sharing opportunities. This includes learning what to do, whom to contact, how to handle different processes, etc. Through this process, the outgoing officer gains valuable management skills and helps strengthen the competence and comfort level of the elected officer. Training that is educational, collaborative, and focused on clear communication adds significant value to the organization.

6.3.2.4 Term Limits

To allow opportunities for others to obtain leadership roles, it is important to define term limits. This greatly reduces the chances of stagnation and helps strengthen overall morale from term to term. Some organizations select 1-2 years as their term limits. In my experience, the preference has been for a single year term limit and here is why:

Typically when you have President-Elect, President, and Past President positions, the President-Elect must pass through a full cycle carrying each of these titles over the course of time. If the term limit is one year, their Presidential tenure will last for three years: one year each for Elect; Current; and Past Presidential roles. If the term limit is two years, you are looking at a total Presidential tenure of six years: two years each for Elect; Current; and Past President roles. A 6-year leadership commitment is a lot to ask of anyone, which is why single year terms are more desirable.[8]

6.3.3 TRANSFERRING CONTACT INFORMATION

When your organizational leadership turns over, the current officers should meet with the officer elects to share contact information. This is usually done at the end of the officer term. Officers should maintain a database with contact information of anyone who has worked with the organization in any way. Due to the sensitive nature of this document, it should be carefully managed. The list should include separate columns for the following: last name; first name; title; email address; phone number; and the nature of the relationship with the organization. This database can be easily made and managed in Excel or Google Sheets.

6.3.4 WORKING IN GOOGLE DRIVE

To soften new officer transition, your contact information database should be carefully explained and passed on to the new leadership team members. One way to improve efficiency is to create a folder in Google Drive. If you have existing Excel files, you can upload and convert them to Google Drive format.[9]

---

8 This is especially the case with voluntary commitments.

9 Greenough, P. D. (2015, July 25). How to Convert an Excel File into a Google Sheet. Retrieved April 20, 2016, from https://www.patrickgreenough.com.

S E C R E T   6 :   S T R A T E G I C   P L A N N I N G

6.3.4.1 *File Structure and Accessibility*

The primary folder should be titled with the same name as your organization. In that file, create sub folders for specific categories of information, each with unique permission sets. Many of these folders should be shared with everyone, but at least one should be shared with only one person. Here is an example of file structure:

>**Folder**: *[Organization Name]*

>**Sub Folder:** *Board Shared Folder* – Accessed and managed by all current board members. Only current board members should have access to this folder, and they should have editing permissions so they can interact where necessary. The following example lists folders that could be housed within this sub folder:

* **Folders**
  o *Board Position Descriptions:* Separate documents explaining each position.
  o *Board Roster Contact Information:* Single Google Sheet document with multiple sheets, one sheet for each board term, and each sheet with columns for last name, first name, position, phone (optional), and email address.
  o *Budget & Financial:* Balance Sheets, Profit & Loss (P&L) Statements, and any other finance related documents.
  o *Area Folders (Collegiate Relations, Communications, etc.):* Individual folders designated for content related to the respective areas.
  o *Logos:* Descriptive.
  o *Marketing Collateral:* Archive collateral designs from previous events to help future boards benchmark with past campaigns.
  o *Meetings:* Meeting minutes and agendas.
  o *Photos:* Descriptive.
  o *Strategic Planning:* Any notes taken at annual board retreats.
  o *Volunteers:* Single spreadsheet with columns for last name, first name, phone (optional), email, and area interest to help facilitate optimal placement.

>**Sub Folder:** *Technology* – Accessed and managed by only one current board member, preferably VP of Technology, and that person should have ownership permissions.[10] This folder holds a single Google Sheet that lists all account login credentials associated with the organization, including email, website hosting, FTP, banking, PayPal, etc. Due to the highly sensitive nature of this document and to prevent account vulnerabilities, only one person on the board should manage this file.

6.3.4.2 File Organization

It is important to note how Google organizes file names in Drive. When using numbers such as dates you should put the full year first, put a zero (0) in front of single-digit months, and leave day as is. The 0 in front of single-digit months is important when you have documents labeled for each month past 9 months. The number 1 comes before 2, but the number 11 does not come before 2. Google will put 2 after 11 because the first digit in 11 is 1 and Google curates document names in Drive based on the first character in a line of syntax. To ensure that all documents are listed in order, make sure to put a 0 in front of months 1-9. For clarity, here is an example:

Let's say I have the following three documents:

*   2014-5-31 P&L Statement
*   2014-2-28 Balance Sheet
*   2014-11-30 Balance Sheet

Google will organize these documents like this:

*   2014-11-30 Balance Sheet
*   2014-2-28 Balance Sheet
*   2014-5-31 P&L Statement

---

10 Prevent risk entirely by ensuring that only one VP can access and manage this document. Some student organizations may allow this document to be accessed by the President, but it should be clearly communicated that only the document manager can modify it, and the President must agree not to revise any of the information without permission from the document manager. This is mission critical!

Obviously, that is incorrect file organization; so let's add a 0 in front of the two files with single-digit month designations to correct it. Google will now organize my files correctly:

* 2014-02-28 Balance Sheet
* 2014-05-31 P&L Statement
* 2014-11-30 Balance Sheet

SUMMARY AND APPLICATIONS TO ENTREPRENEURSHIP

This Secret provides an introduction to strategic planning for your student organization. This includes complete instructions for how to implement the World Café, a conversational process that provides a better understanding of how to best utilize resources. This process should be done on a frequently lenient but routine basis, preferably annually. This Secret also provides guidance for potential topics to discuss during an Executive Retreat, also preferably done at least annually. Action items for this meeting should include: Constitution and Bylaws; vision; mission; values; objectives; SWOT Analysis; yearly goals; officer roles; succession planning; and the election process. Finally, one way to archive files is to create a folder in Google Drive, provide the proper permissions where necessary, and acknowledge Google's organization logic.

For the remainder of this Secret, we will take our knowledge of student organization strategic planning and apply it to business.

6.4 PLANNING STAFF MEETINGS

Strategic planning is an integral process for business. It helps build and strengthen a team-building atmosphere, brings clarity to resource allocation, and enhances alignment between the values of the individual and the organization as a whole. Also, it fosters opportunities to augment communication and relationships between team members. When running your business, you should meet with your executive staff to discuss the progress objectives associated with your organization. While common intervals are weekly or monthly, you should select meeting times, durations, and frequencies that accommodate the working style and objectives. Meetings do not have to be regularly scheduled. When you do have them, however, the focus should be about keeping the team current with project progress and allow for a medium to openly discuss problems or issues so the team can collectively decide on how to steer the project.

Your executive staff meetings should be scheduled at least one week in advance with open durations but not exceeding one hour. Ideal meeting days are either Mondays or Tuesdays because, in many professional environments, the weekly workload tends to pick up after Tuesday. This is just one strategy. Decide on a method that works for your team and plan accordingly. There is no wrong answer; it just depends on your preference.

6.5 SCHEDULING

6.5.1 WORKING REMOTELY

If your employees work remotely, use a software program to identify the best meeting time for everyone. One such program is Doodle.

Once everyone has contributed to the Doodle with indications of preferred times, you should schedule a conference call. For efficiency, you should consider sending the reminders out as email calendar invitations. When a calendar invitation is received, it allows the recipient to indicate his or her attendance commitment: Yes; No; or Maybe and his or her response is automatically added to his or her email calendar. This is a very simple process and prevents busy professionals from having to manually input information into their calendars, which is tedious and inefficient.

6.5.2 WORKING LOCALLY

If your employees work centrally together out of the same building, you might consider inviting everyone to meet in a reserved room. If you plan to meet regularly, make sure to schedule a running room reservation. Meeting attendance should be mandatory.[11] For the sake of efficiency, reconsider having a meeting if there are no pressing items to discuss. Do not meet for the sake of meeting; it is a waste of time.[12]

---

11 Attendance should be mandatory for only those whose work is directly affected by the items discussed in the meeting.

12 Having regularly scheduled meetings for the sake of having regularly scheduled meetings is a common blunder among many teams. Unless there's a pressing emergency or there's something that simply cannot be resolved any other way, there's really no need to have a meeting.

6.6 CREATING AGENDAS & MEETING MINUTES
6.6.1 STAFF MEETINGS:
Agenda Required; Minutes Optional

A meeting agenda acts as a helpful reference for attendees. Agendas should be made ahead of time and passed out at the beginning of the meetings. Since you will be working off this document, everyone should have a copy before the meeting starts. Printed agendas should have some blank space to allow for note taking during meetings. Meeting minutes may not be necessary.

6.6.2 STEERING COMMITTEE MEETINGS:
Agenda Required; Minutes Required

In addition to meeting agendas, minutes should always be recorded for high-profile meetings that take place on a more reduced frequency. Depending on the nature of the committee, these meetings should occur monthly, quarterly, bi-annually, or annually. The following is a brief list of events where meeting minutes should always be recorded:

*   Advisory Board Meetings
*   Board of Directors Meetings
*   Executive Committee Meetings
*   Planning Committee Meetings
*   Executive Retreats

These are all program and/or event steering committees and some of these group names are or can be synonymous with one another. Because each of these groups is typically made up of executive-level people, these meetings should be carefully and strategically planned, implemented, and recorded.

6.6.3 MEETING MINUTES
Minutes should be carefully recorded by the Secretary or assigned party and reviewed and approved by the Advisory Board members before distributing them to group members. The minutes should be sent out after the meeting

concludes and by the end of the same week as the meeting. When sending out the meeting minutes, specific language should be included in the message indicating a request for the recipient to review the minutes for accuracy and to provide feedback. Requesting the feedback by a stated future date will emphasize urgency. The approval of the meeting minutes from the most recent meeting should be the first action item on the agenda for your next meeting.

6.7 CONDUCTING MEETINGS
6.7.1 FOLLOWING ROBERT'S RULES OF ORDER

For a more formal approach to conducting meetings, you might review the literature associated with Robert's Rules of Order. These rules explain how to carry out concisely structured meetings. While not required, it is nice to have this kind of perspective on how to conduct your meetings. This includes establishing a quorum size and deciding on how many members must be present to conduct a meeting and pass a motion.

PART II

Part II covers Income Generation, Branding, Marketing, and Website Development. Each of these concepts is covered in its own unique Secret. Due to the complex nature of these Secrets, applications to entrepreneurship are discussed throughout.

Secret 7

GENERATING INCOME

Student organizations should be run in a way that focuses on adding value to its members. Student organization involvement should come at little to no cost to its members. A membership fee is typically required when the organization is a collegiate affiliate of a national brand such as the American Marketing Association, or Net Impact. Non-affiliate, student-built brands do not always require membership fees. Some of them offer some form of non-monetary membership requirement such as minimum GPA, or letter of recommendation. Many student organizations are not as focused on profit as much as value even if a financial requirement exists. However, for those organizations that do want to produce revenue, this Secret will come in handy.

The student organization should be run like a business. There are many ways to monetize your student or professional organization. In this section, we will discuss some options you can use to accomplish that.

7.1 UNDERSTANDING MEMBERSHIP FEES

You should arrange a membership fee structure that stimulates profit growth. You can use these added funds for expenses related to your organization such as venue reservations, speaker compensations, and travel expenses. If you run a collegiate chapter of the American Marketing Association (AMA), students will have to pay a fee to become members of the organization itself, in addition to any fee associated with the collegiate chapter (where applicable).[1] Here is what that might look like:

* National American Marketing Association membership fee: $47
* Collegiate chapter membership fee: [$X][2]
* **Total cost** to become a member of the collegiate chapter of the American Marketing Association: [**$X**]

If you operate a professional affiliate of a national organization that requires its members to pay a fee to become members at the national level, you can add an extra fee in addition to becoming members at the affiliate level.[3] Let's consider the following structure setup again for the American Marketing Association but this time with regard to a professional affiliate:[4]

* National membership fee: $220
* Los Angeles affiliate membership fee: $70
* **Total cost** to become a member of the Los Angeles affiliate of the American Marketing Association: **$290**

If you operate an affiliate, your affiliate membership fee acts as operating profit. If you are the founder of an organization unassociated with a national structure, you can create a fee structure at your discretion. It is important to consider a fee that is relevant to your service offerings. To get an idea of a realistic and convertible fee, you should conduct a brief competitor analysis for review of membership pricing structures offered by competing organizations. If a competing organization is charging $45 and offers similar services but in a different category, you should use that number as a benchmark and

---

1 Student. (n.d.). Retrieved April 20, 2016, from https://www.ama.org.

2 "X" is used to symbolize whatever cost is decided and totaled.

3 Professional Chapters. (n.d.). Retrieved April 20, 2016, from https://www.ama.org.

4 Los Angeles is used as an example. These fees may be subject to change. The professional affiliate fee will vary depending on location.

SECRET 7: GENERATING INCOME

compare it with the service offerings your organization provides and adjust accordingly.[5]

If you feel your organization offers more or superior services than a competing organization that charges $45, you might consider charging more. You could also charge slightly less, i.e., $40, with the intention of offering a better product at a better price. This strategy can be useful in some ways but if used to an extreme degree, say with a significantly reduced price tag, it can damage brand credibility. Price can influence consumers' perception of value associated with a brand.

7.1.1 OFFERING MEMBERSHIP TIERS & VALUE OPPORTUNITIES

Your student organization can be perceived as higher quality if it offers multiple layers of quality. Here are two ways that illustrate how:

1. **Your student organization offers multiple levels of membership:** If each level is offered at different price points, prospective members may view the higher priced membership tier as the superior option.[6] Another example is when your organization offers tier level sponsorship options, i.e., bronze, silver, gold, platinum, etc., each with a higher price and more robust accommodations than the last. In this case, where accommodations are spelled out, price will be associated with value.

2. **Your student organization offers more value opportunities in comparison to competing student organizations:** If more value is offered, your members may view your organization with higher esteem.[7] For example, if your organization offers resume workshops and networking opportunities with executives in addition to membership status

---

5 For a discussion on how to identify value and fee structure, refer to sections 1.2.2 and 1.2.3.

6 While the membership tier structure can be utilized by student organizations, it is more commonly found in professional organizations.

7 More value offered does not always equate to higher esteem. For example, large public discount retailers may offer more value but may also have lower overall esteem when compared to small private retailers.

and regularly scheduled meetings, and the competing organization only offers membership status and regularly scheduled meetings, your organization may be perceived as more desirable.

These are specific examples to consider when planning your membership pricing structure. An optimal balance of benefits and price will enhance the desire for the prospective member to accept your membership fee structure and reject that of the competing organization. Once you select a membership fee structure, commit to it until there is an identifiable need to change it.[8]

7.2 IMPLEMENTING LARGE-SCALE NETWORKING EVENTS

This section caters more to the organization as big business. The focus in this section is on making money, and the figures are large but not unrealistic for professional organizations. For student organization programming, the focus should be on finding ways to do it at little to no cost as discussed in Secret 5. Additionally, large-scale networking events are not commonly found in many student organizations due to the rigorous time commitment required for planning. Student organizations are included in our discussion for those interested in implementing one of these types of events.

It is beneficial to think about how an organization can be run like a business. Large-scale networking events can be robust income producing activities. These events have other benefits as well, which can include forming new relationships with vendors, providing valuable networking events to members, and learning the implementation process for larger scaled events. For this discussion, we will focus specifically on the monetization model for large-scale networking events.

There are many different ways to structure large-scale networking events. The following strategies are provided to show you how to keep your costs down. The idea is to grow your profit margin.

---

8 Price adjustment occurs for many reasons including demand increase or supply decrease. Whatever the case, be aware of what circumstances require a fee adjustment and implement accordingly.

7.2.1 SELECTING DATE AND VENUE

For student organizations, find a conference room on campus. Investigate the reservation requirements. Many campuses only require a significant lead-time for preparation and planning; sometimes this could mean 8-12 months in advance. Your reservation may require you to provide a minimal amount of information such as anticipated attendance yield. This will allow the institution to provide accurate accommodations. Whatever the case, secure a date and venue first before you tackle anything else.

For businesses, if there are conferences in your area, follow up with the vendors associated with providing the space. Hotels are popular business conference venue spaces. Check the hotels in your area for possible conference room reservation opportunities. Because this is a business-to-business (B2B) arrangement, your reservation will likely be associated with an expense. Talk to the vendor and see if a trade partnership can be arranged in the hope of securing the venue complimentarily. One strategy could be to invite the vendor to co-sponsor the event with you. In this way, you could market the vendor on your website and in any marketing collateral associated with the event. To make the deal even more attractive, offer a profit sharing opportunity. In the case of a profit share, the vendor will take a percentage of the revenue generated from each event registration. Here is an example:

* Event registration fee: $400
* Conference room capacity: 500
* Profit sharing ratio: 25/75 (25% for the vendor; 75% for your organization)
* Revenue sharing capacity: $50,000 for your vendor; $150,000 for your organization

With those variables, the vendor will receive $100, and you will receive $300 for each registered attendee. If the conference room sells out, the total profit generated for the vendor would be $50,000. That number may be slightly lower if you are offering complimentary registration for any of your attendees. Offering complimentary registrations is not uncommon but typically reserved for high-level executives, guest speakers, and premium sponsors.

It may seem $50,000 is a lot of money to give away to secure a conference room at a five-star hotel. Keep in mind that depending on where you reserve your room, the reservation cost may exceed $50,000. Costs commonly associated with this fee may include parking, dining, setup, breakdown, employee compensation, and sometimes even security. Conference planning is highly complex logistically so if you plan on having a conversation about trade sponsorship, be prepared to discuss an arrangement that will be attractive to the vendor.

Other venue options could be something as casual as reserving space at a local upscale bar. Choose something nice, perhaps a rooftop location or lounge. Be selective because the venue will reflect the brand of your organization or company. Often these reservations come at a very minimal cost if any at all. Sometimes there is a spending minimum. For example, reservations can be made as long as there is a commitment that your organization will spend a certain amount of money on food and drinks during your event. This spending minimum, or cover, is generally reasonable but be sure to inquire about this during your first interaction with the venue so that you can plan accordingly. Depending on your expected attendance outcome and type of event you are planning, these locations may make great alternatives.[9]

7.2.2 PLANNING EVENT STRUCTURES

In this section, we will discuss different types and structures of large-scale networking events. The following list is not cumulative but is provided to give you an idea of events in this category.

7.2.2.1 *Award Ceremonies*

One example is the Marketer of the Year (M.O.Y.) Awards. This event gives credit to a short list of local marketers who have made a significant positive impact on their community. One marketer is selected by the event planning committee to be the recipient of the award. Planning for an award ceremony

---

9 These alternative locations cater more to the professional networking event. Event logistics are usually more simplified and required reservation lead-times are generally significantly shorter.

should start at least 8 months in advance and marketing should start at least 6 months in advance. The target market for this event should be the audiences for your organization, any partnering organizations, and any sponsors.

Additional structure to this event consists of gathering donations from local vendors and auctioning them off with all proceeds going to your organization or business. In return for this income stream, you should promote all vendors who donated the items for the auctions. Give credit where credit is due.

7.2.2.2 Fundraiser, Charity, and Gala Events

These events are provided to promote and support some stated initiative or fund, i.e., scholarship fund, disease research fund, etc. These are usually black-tie events and include formal dinner accommodations. High-level speakers and auctions are typically provided. This type of event can easily be coupled with an award ceremony. If your organization is aiming to stimulate funding for some initiative that will benefit your members and the community, this is an option to consider.

7.2.2.3 Conferences

Conferences are themed events specific to some topic within an industry. High-level industry executives commonly attend conferences, so audience participation is usually robust. This is one of the primary reasons why you can and should charge a premium for participation.[10]

---

10 For a detailed review of conference design, refer to section 5.3.

SUMMARY AND APPLICATIONS TO ENTREPRENEURSHIP

This Secret provides an overview of unique ways to help your organization or business generate income. The review of membership fees provides a rich understanding of how to create a pricing structure. Focus on creating and offering multiple layers of value to your members. Always aim to give more than just membership status. This may include organizing workshops and professional networking activities. Focus on creating situations where your members can find new opportunities. Large-scale networking events, while not as commonly found in student organizations, are great ways to do this.

Hosting events can help stimulate awareness of your organization or business. This is especially valuable if your organization or business is brand new. Arrange trade partnerships with venue providers with the specific intention of acquiring room reservations complimentarily. While this may not be possible, you should at least try. In discussions, be prepared to offer trade arrangements that are highly attractive to vendors. Strongly consider including profit sharing options.

Organizations should be run like businesses. This is integral for sustainability. Focus on developing new ways to generate income for your organization. Whatever funds are generated should be funneled right back into your organization to stimulate additional growth and development opportunities. Repeat this process for the life of the organization.

Secret 8

BRANDING

This Secret covers how to brand your student organization. This includes logo design and market positioning.

8.1 CREATING YOUR LOGO

Consider two definitions: brand image, and brand identity. The brand image is how the market perceives your brand. In contrast, the brand identity is how your brand wants to be perceived by the market. The goal is parallel alignment of the brand identity and brand image.

It is very important to select the right logo the first time. Once the logo is selected, your organization should be prepared to commit to using it for the life of the organization. Once a logo is created and used, it generates associations within the minds of the consumer, which forms the brand image. In the case of the student organization, the consumers are the students, faculty, and staff. Care should be taken in the logo selection process. It is relatively easy to create a brand image, but it is somewhat difficult to change it after the fact.

8.1.1 DESIGNING YOUR LOGO

Your logo should reflect the strategic direction of your organization. For example, if your organization were about astronomy, it would make sense to have an image of a planet or star in your logo instead of a skateboarder or baseball player. If your organization targets math students, it would make sense to have numbers in your logo instead of non-related symbols, characters, or images. These are just some ideas. Make logo distinction easily identifiable.

Another nice idea, if possible, is incorporating the logo of your academic institution with your logo. You will need permission before you employ this concept. Start first by contacting your Student Affairs/Activities Office and go from there.[1]

8.1.2 OUTSOURCING LOGO DESIGN WORK

If you do not possess the proper equipment or skills to draft a final version of your logo, you might consider sourcing this task to a third party. For new student organizations, start first with your own network. See if there is anyone who has the skills required to produce your logo. This is a great opportunity to form a partnership. It could be a monetary or trade partnership. You can provide financial compensation or offer something of fair value in return. For example, if you hire a student to design your logo, you might consider offering them complimentary single-term membership to your organization as a trade for their services. Additionally, this student could be the point person for marketing collateral materials or even a potential officer.

If you are unsuccessful in your attempts to find someone in your network that can draft your final logo, find a business that does print design and schedule an appointment. If your organization is already monetized, you may use existing funds to pay for this service. Here are some places where you can find related services:

* **LogoBee**, **LogoDesignCreation:** Logo design companies
* **Upwork**: Great place to find freelancers
* **FASTSIGNS:** Have a banner or sign made that displays your logo

---

1 Student Affairs/Activities Center is covered in section 4.1.

8.1.3 SELECTING YOUR LOGO

If you run an existing student organization and intend to implement a rebrand, involve your members in the process and invite them to submit their concept ideas by a stated date. Once enough submissions are acquired, there are two ways to select a final logo:

1. **Executive Committee selects final logo:** To prevent a response bias, any executive committee members that submitted a logo should not be included in the logo selection process.

2. **Member's select final logo:** Send out a message to all members with a link to a webpage that houses each of the submitted logos with numbers assigned to each. In the same message include a link to a SurveyMonkey or Google Forms survey with all of the logo numbers listed on the survey. Set up the survey so that it allows for only one response per voter. Invite the members to vote on the logo they like the most by some stated date. Follow these rules to prevent a response bias:

   o Do not credit the logo designers on the webpage that depicts the logos.

   o Do not send the voter message to any of the logo designers.

8.1.4 PLACING YOUR LOGO

When your logo is created, put it on all marketing collateral materials that involve your organization. Examples include: sign-in sheets; invitations; flyers; banners; stickers; and social media profiles.[2] This list can get pretty lengthy but is important to stimulate and strengthen market visibility and awareness. Be careful not to be seen as a content spammer. Market your brand only where necessary and when it makes sense. If your organization is involved in an event or process, it makes sense. Depending on the message you wish to relay to your target audience, plastering your stickers all over the property just for the sake of entertainment can damage your brand image. Be sensible about where, when, and how you place your logo.

---

2 Social Media is covered in section 9.4.

8.2 MARKET POSITIONING

Brand positioning is about identity manipulation. You want to position your brand so it helps guide the consumer to perceive the brand in a way that is more aligned with the brand identity. To position your organization's brand, understand how your organization is currently perceived and compare it with how you would like it to be perceived. In other words, compare your brand image with your brand identity. From there, act accordingly to make the necessary changes to stimulate closer alignment of these two concepts.

8.2.1 POSITIONING NEW ORGANIZATIONS

For newly minted student organizations, the executive team should decide on what characteristics make up the brand identity. This concept should be the core of any marketing initiatives. This will enable the organization to strengthen the possibility of forming the intended brand image. For example, if the organization is intended to provide networking opportunities for students, it should plan to host at least one significant, well-marketed, and well-attended networking event per term. Do this consistently to better align your brand image and brand identity.

8.2.2 POSITIONING EXISTING ORGANIZATIONS

For existing organizations, the executive team should identify how they want the organization to be perceived and immediately identify ways to make any necessary changes to the brand image. For example, if your organization targets math students but for some reason is attracting accounting students, find out why and then investigate opportunities to strategically position your organization for math students. This might be in the form of scheduling appearances at, or hosting, math tutoring sessions.

8.2.3 USING AND MISUSING ACRONYMS

To ensure a consistent alignment of your brand identity and brand image, it is important to acknowledge the significance associated with stating your brand name in full every single time. The minute you begin using an acronym to reference your brand is the minute this alignment weakens. There is one exception to this rule, and it exists when the brand name consists of a series of complicated words.[3] In this special case, you might consider re-branding by way of acronym to save your audience time and make it easier for them to remember the name. If this strategy is adopted, pick an acronym that makes up a word that is also associated with the brand.

SUMMARY AND APPLICATIONS TO ENTREPRENEURSHIP

Selecting the right logo for your student organization is integral to the development and sustainability of your brand. The logo should reflect your brand identity and should be marketed strategically. The final design may be done by someone in your network, or sourced out if not done by you. For existing organizations that intend to implement a rebrand, involve your members in the process and do what you can to avoid a response bias. Marketing initiatives and logo placement should be done carefully and strategically to augment the brand image.

Market positioning is a careful procedure that should be strategically maintained. By comparing your brand image with your brand identity, you can better understand where to make changes to improve the alignment of these two factors. This should be investigated as early as possible during the life of the organization and should be properly managed on a regular basis. Additionally, the use of acronyms should be carefully examined. While it is ideal to refrain from using them to ensure a strong alignment between the brand identity and the brand image, it may be an improvement opportunity if the acronym helps the target market more quickly gain an association with your brand. This can be especially useful when the acronym makes up a word associated with the brand.

---

3 Acronyms are commonly used in industries such as the military, operations, and project management but the use of acronyms in these cases generally applies to process and application names.

Secret 9

MARKETING

Marketing is a contest for attention. The company that has the most attention, or eyes looking at it, usually wins. To win that attention, you must focus on adding value to your target audience. This Secret covers how to market your student organization. While we will be discussing word-of-mouth, and print marketing strategies, the majority of the conversation will be about email and online marketing strategies.

> Marketing is about attracting eyes to your product or service.

Direct marketing is a very common approach to enhancing brand awareness, and it occurs when you provide information about your services straight to potential and existing customers. You see this with physical mail when you receive newspaper-like ads for discounts on items at your local grocery store or political promotional materials during election time. In the case of student organizations, your direct marketing typically occurs in the form of classroom pitches[1], word-of-mouth, print, email and online marketing.

---

1 Pitching to classrooms is covered in section 3.1.

9.1 WORD-OF-MOUTH MARKETING

This occurs when people talk about your brand. A great way to stimulate discussion is to do something very robust in the beginning. This might be a large networking event, co-sponsoring an event with another student organization, running an entertaining but educational contest, etc. If you do something that stimulates a lot of traffic and activity early on, people are more likely to talk about it within their networks. This can be very beneficial for member growth and student organization sustainability.

One of the many advantages to word-of-mouth marketing is that those people who talk about your brand do a lot of the marketing for you. This can be very powerful if you have a great product or service that people like.

9.2 PRINT MARKETING

Print is slowly losing its popularity and relevance in the marketplace due to the advent of online marketing. While it is not nearly as prominent as it once was in years past, it still carries some degree of importance in your marketing mix.[2] If your campus has a daily press, consider running an advertisement in it to take advantage of this medium. Also, check to see if there are newsletter opportunities. If you can swing it financially, check your local newspaper for price points. A lot of times, local companies have a natural inclination to give back to local universities, so you might be surprised at what kinds of accommodations these contacts can provide. Either way, this is a great way to build relationships with internal and external vendors.

9.3 EMAIL MARKETING

If done strategically, email marketing can be very effective at driving traffic to an event. The goal with email marketing is to increase conversion rates.[3] Common prompted actions are product purchases or event RSVPs. If your

---

2 The marketing mix consists of the Four Ps: Product; Price; Place, and Promotion. This includes: what it is; how much you will charge for it; and where and how you will market it.

3 A conversion rate is the proportion of visitors that take some specific form of action as directed by the marketer.

student organization is hosting an event and you want to send an invitation to your student email list, which you have gathered from previously hosted events, it is important to consider how to craft your message to increase its visibility.

The only way to ensure that your email has a chance of stimulating conversions is if it dodges common spam filters and makes it to the recipient's inbox. To avoid the spam filters, carefully consider what words you include in the subject line. There is an abundant list of spam trigger words to avoid in a helpful article on hubspot.com.[4]

9.3.1 CRAFTING YOUR MESSAGE

After you have carefully constructed your email subject line, you can write the body of your message. Care should be taken in how you construct the body. You want to convey just the right amount of information without being seen as too salesy, or spammy. Your goal is to increase conversion rates. Doing that requires a bit of finesse when it comes to email marketing. The following is a list of key points to consider when drafting an email. Aim to utilize these methods in your messages. There are limitless ways to do this via multimedia, or just plain text.

* **Value proposition:** Let the recipients know, in a very clear way, how or why your service or product will positively impact their lives.
* **Sense of urgency:** Indicate that the recipients should act now to reserve their spot. This will help stimulate the recipients to take action. Common language includes: Limited Spaces, or Limited Time.
* **Call-to-Action (CTA):** There should be several places in your message that provide robust calls to action. Some examples of common key phrases include: Buy Now; RSVP; Sign Me Up; and Order Now.

9.3.2 IMPLEMENTING YOUR STRATEGY

There are many strategies to utilize to implement an email marketing campaign. Some of these strategies are listed here. The goal is to increase click-through

---

4 Rubin, K. (2012, January 11). The Ultimate List of Email SPAM Trigger Words. Retrieved April 20, 2016, from http://blog.hubspot.com.

rates (CTRs) and ultimately conversions. In doing so, you should aim to build brand loyalty.

Strategy #1: **Email Drip Marketing Leading Up to the Event**

Choice can be demotivating, so it is in your best interest to position each of your emails to request only one action.[5] Consider this when drafting newsletter-type emails. Broadcast only one action, or one choice, at a time. For event planning, each email should provide valuable information pertaining to the event and a call to action to stimulate registration as the single choice per email. The more value your event provides, the better your chances of driving registrations. You can use promo codes to offer Early Bird registrations. You can create promo codes at eventbrite.com.[6]

The following is a list of items to consider when implementing email-marketing campaigns for your events. When to start your email-marketing campaign depends on the structure and complexity of your event.[7] Each email should have links to your website and social media channels.[8] Calls for Early Bird registration should be introduced early in the campaign.[9] Each email leading up to the event should be sent more than once to drive awareness and build momentum.

*   **Event Teaser.** This email is sent before a date is selected but with the intention of letting the recipient know this event will take place at some point in the relatively near future. The purpose is to build awareness. The structure of this email could be a simple, straightforward message and nothing more.

---

5 Ciotti, G. (n.d.). 3 Strategies To Get Responses To Your Emails. Retrieved April 20, 2016, from https://blog.aweber.com.

6 Eventbrite Customer Experience Team. (2015, September 23). How to apply a discount or access code to your order. Retrieved April 20, 2016, from https://www.eventbrite.com.

7 Influential factors may include: number of speakers; breakout sessions; target market; and food procurement.

8 Throughout the duration of your campaign, utilize social media to share reminders and information about the speakers and content related to the event offerings.

9 Early emails should clearly state the promo code activation deadline for Early Bird registration. After the deadline has passed, any additional emails should state the regular registration rate.

* **Save the Date.** This email is sent when a date has been selected. This message will include the event title and date. If you plan to host a keynote speaker, you might include a professional headshot, brief bio, and a short description of the speech. State the date and indicate more details are to come. An efficient way to promote this email is to send it as a calendar invitation.
* **Event Information & Agenda.** This email should include all the necessary information regarding the event including full speaker roster, detailed agenda, time and place, parking information including associated fees, etc.
* **Reminder of Value Offered.** This email should remind attendees of the value the event will provide. This could include networking opportunities, rare face time with top executives, and category education.
* **Venue Location, Map, and Parking.** This email should include venue location and parking with associated fees where necessary. This email should be sent a few days before the event and again the night before as a final reminder.
* **The Day After the Event:** Send a Thank You letter to your email list thanking them for attending the event. Keep this email very brief. Even if not everyone on your email list attended the event, those who did will appreciate this brief gesture. See Figure 9.1 for an example:

Dear [Name],

Thank you for attending our event. We hope you enjoyed it, and we look forward to seeing you at the next one.

[Your full name (more personal) or business name]

Figure 9.1: Thank You email to send out after event conclusion

Strategy #2: **Separate Converts from Prospects**

You have two types of clients, and each has a unique way with money. The difference between prospective clients and existing clients is that one costs you money while the other makes you money, respectively.[10] Regarding student

---

10 Reeves, J. (2013, July 03). 3 Advanced Email Marketing Strategies Guaranteed To Grow Your Business. Retrieved April 20, 2016, from http://blog.crazyegg.com.

SECRET 9: MARKETING

organizations, you have prospective, and existing members. You should separate these groups into their own lists and market to each one uniquely. Prospective list marketing should be done to entice conversions. You can do this by sending reminders to your prospective list indicating why your service is important and how the prospective members can benefit from it. Marketing to the existing member list is done differently. Treat this like a list of your closest friends. You should offer these members exclusive deals, and specials to strengthen brand loyalty and to keep them coming back as repeat attendees, or repeat customers.

Strategy #3: **The Urgency Approach**

Urgency is a great motivator. If something is time sensitive, it has a way of crippling procrastination. This is especially true with email marketing. If you position the content in your email message as beneficial if acted upon by a certain date or time, say with the provision of a discount on a future registration, or a free offer, you can assume a stronger potential for a higher number of respondents. Make sure that if offered, the freebie is of relevant value to the recipient. Otherwise, you risk hurting the brand image. For example, if your goal is to drive respondents to a product pre-sale reservation, you might use language similar to the following:

* *Reserve your copy by [date] and receive a [%] discount*
* *Reserve your copy by [date] and receive a free complimentary [item]*

These are just two examples used to help prompt the act of taking action.

9.3.3 DEVELOPING AND MANAGING YOUR EMAIL ADDRESS LIST DATABASE

There are many ways to capture email addresses. Some common methods are listed here:

9.3.3.1 *Event Sign-In Sheets:*

At events, request that all attendees print their name and provide their email addresses on some pre-structured sign-in sheet. This is a great way to capture email addresses because it is a simple, low-stress request from event attendees. An added benefit is the sign-in sheet helps you track attendance numbers.[11]

9.3.3.2 Raffles:

If you host a raffle at an event, pass around a box or jar and ask attendees to drop their business cards in it for a chance to win a raffle prize. For student organization events, ask students to put their names and emails on small pieces of paper to be dropped into the box or jar. This is another very simple but effective way to capture attendee information. For business events and depending on how much information you request on the sign-in sheet, this approach might be more robust given that many business cards are more information-rich.

9.3.3.3 Opt-In Pages (Squeeze Pages):

This is a powerful method and might be the most efficient. When you visit a website, and a window pops up requesting you to submit an email address to receive something free in return, you are doing what is called, "opting in." What this means is that you are freely providing the website managers with the opportunity to market directly to you. These pages are called Squeeze Pages.

For student organization leaders, see if your university offers a way to use a school-branded web page. This would be highly advantageous for increasing visibility to your target audience. If this opportunity exists, see if you are allowed to create an opt-in form on that page so that interested students can submit their emails. Set it up so that when an email is submitted, the student is automatically sent an email invitation to the next event, or a PDF with resources related to the theme of your organization. For example, if you are running a student organization at the business school, the PDF might have information on how to dress for an interview. Inquire about this with your Student Affairs/Activity Center and plan accordingly.[12]

---

11 For sign-in sheet design, refer to section 3.1.5.

12 Student Affairs/Activities Center is covered in section 4.1.

For company owners, your website has a higher chance of retrieving email addresses this way if you are giving away something of value to the prospective consumer in trade. A common example is to set up your squeeze page to automatically send the subscriber a downloadable resource when he or she submits his or her email address. They give you something, and you give them something in return.

9.3.3.4 *Webinars:*

Hosting webinars is another great way to build your email list. An easy way to drive traffic to a squeeze page that markets a webinar is to use one of the social media advertising platforms, preferably Facebook due to its dominant market reach. The squeeze page should indicate the title and date of the webinar and any guest speakers where applicable. Ideally, anyone who wishes to attend the webinar is required to submit his or her email address. When they do this, you capture his or her email address, and they are automatically sent webinar reservation information.

Find a place to store, organize and use your captured email addresses. Here are some options to consider:

* **AWeber**: Email Marketing software
* **Constant Contact**: Email campaigns
* **CVENT**: Event and list management
* **InfusionSoft**: Small business marketing software
* **MailChimp**: Email campaigns

In Internet marketing, email lists can be organized into many different groups or segments. If organized and used strategically and with the strict intention of adding value, larger lists should increase conversion potential, which is discussed in the following section.

9.3.4 MARKETING TO AN EMAIL LIST

For student organizations, the conversion rate is the percentage of email subscribers that RSVPs to an event. A large attendee turnout can enhance networking opportunities, which can help strengthen the total value potential of the event. Also, you will be better able to share the value of the event with more students at one time. For businesses, the conversion rate is the percentage of email subscribers that purchase your product. This can greatly influence your income potential.

Let's say your product is finally complete and you are ready to monetize. Ideally, your product should be available to purchase online. The link to your product purchase page is what you send to your email list in the form of a sales letter. The larger the list, the better chances for conversion rates and ultimately generating a passive revenue stream. Here is an example with parameters to give you an idea of how this works:

* Your email list size: 50,000
* Price point for your product: $97
* Conversion rate: 2%
* Total revenue: (50000 x .02) x $97 = **$97,000**

Your revenue stream with these parameters is $97,000![13] This is just with a 2% conversion rate. If your product yields a higher conversion rate, the total revenue only gets bigger. Do this once a month and you can see the massive income potential. This is very powerful. The money is in the list. Focus your efforts on creating a valuable product and growing your email list.

9.3.5 OBEYING CAN-SPAM LAWS

You should use your email list very carefully. Do not abuse it. You are handling private information, and there are rules associated with how to use it. The CAN-SPAM Act was setup to police how commercial emails are marketed. The Federal Trade Commission (FTC) showcases the following CAN-SPAM requirements and indicates that each single email in violation is subject to fines of up to $16,000.[14]

---

13 This figure will vary depending on list size, price point, and conversion rate percentage.
14 CAN-SPAM Act: A Compliance Guide for Business. (2009, September). Retrieved April 20, 2016, from https://www.ftc.gov.

* Refrain from using false or misleading header information
* Refrain from using deceptive subject lines
* Clearly indicate that the message is an advertisement
* Be transparent about where you are located
* Be transparent about how subscribers can opt out of receiving future email
* Honor opt-out requests within 10 business days
* Be aware of what others are doing on your behalf

While not indicated in the above section, it is also encouraged to follow proper email privacy protocol. Here is another suggestion to maintain user privacy:

* **Blind Carbon Copy (Bcc):** This is a commonly overlooked method but it is just as important as those methods shared by the FTC. When sending emails to more than one person and the recipients do not know each other, you should always use the Bcc function on these emails. This protects the privacy of all recipients. This is what is commonly referred to as good "netiquette."

9.4 ONLINE MARKETING

Online marketing has garnered significant attention since technology has made Internet access readily available. Online marketing can be an efficient and effective method for marketing. The transition from place to space has become the gold standard for those companies looking to maximize the total value of their marketing campaigns. Online marketing acts as a form of modern front-end customer support. With online marketing, you are interfacing with customers to ensure and maintain customer satisfaction. This includes monitoring the behavior of your audiences. Further, while not required, you are strongly encouraged to be available to your customers on a routine basis. This will allow you to ameliorate customer issues when they arise, which might include: defusing angry customers, and addressing customer complaints. All of this, if handled professionally, will strengthen the brand image of your student organization.

Online marketing has many faces. This section will focus more specifically on social media. Social media is a more robust form of list management.

Instead of just email addresses, you can now build lists of complete customer profiles. Social media has become a significant thread in the fabric of modern marketing. The advent of online communities has allowed companies to better understand the aggregated personalities of their target audiences. Because the method of interaction has changed from a push environment to a listening environment, companies are forced to become more transparent. This has led to better customer service, behavior monitoring on the side of both company and customer, and relationship building that enhances customer loyalty. Let's look at some ways you can use social media to strengthen your brand.

Your online brand should be created with the goal of strengthening customer relationships and increasing conversion rates. This may be in the form of event registrations, product purchases, or some other desired action. For student organizations, focus should be placed on building relationships with students, and inviting them to attend your events. In this section, we will review how to engage your lists on three popular social platforms.[15]

9.4.1 LINKEDIN

LinkedIn is a professional social network. You may think of LinkedIn as an interactive resume. It is best to position yourself on this social network as a professional in whatever you do to make your money. This includes uploading a photo of a professional headshot and keeping your profile up to date. It is important to showcase your skills, education, and professional experience. From there, you can request fellow members you have worked with in the past either professionally or academically to write recommendations and provide endorsements for you. You should return the favor.

For student organization leaders, you will want to create a LinkedIn profile to direct existing and prospective members. Identify which type of LinkedIn profile best suits your student organization, a Company Page or a LinkedIn Group.[16] Both of these options help drive additional marketing but are different formats so

---

15 Social media strategy encompasses an extensive variety of methods with varying levels of complexity. This Secret covers some of the basics to get you started.

16 Ruff, L. (2014, July 6). Building Community with LinkedIn Company Pages vs. LinkedIn Groups. Retrieved April 20, 2016, from https://www.linkedin.com.

identify which one accommodates your working objectives and plan accordingly. See Figure 9.2 for a comparison of key differences between Pages and Groups.

LinkedIn Company Pages	LinkedIn Groups
Optimized for brands	Optimized for communities
Admins generate content; Members and Non-Members can comment, like, and share	Admins and Members can generate content, comment, like, and share
Great option for people who want to keep informed about a business	Great option for people with common interests

Figure 9.2: LinkedIn Company Pages v. LinkedIn Groups

When prospective members inquire about your student organization outside of LinkedIn, you should respond with answers to their questions where applicable, and then re-direct them to your organization's social presence so they can connect with your community.[17] This is a great way to collect member profiles and build your online community. Once they are there, post links that point to your event registration and other landing pages to stimulate conversions. Just like email address list management, the more people you have on your social page, the higher the probability of stimulating more conversions.

9.4.2 FACEBOOK

Facebook is a more casual social network. On Facebook, you are allowed to write more information in your posts, which may help better promote events and stimulate conversions. Additionally, Facebook is great for sharing photos and videos as they can be housed right inside the posts themselves. To optimize your Facebook presence for your organization, create either a Business Page or Group instead of a Profile Page. The main reason is that Facebook has a 5000 friends limit for Profile Pages but allows for unlimited Likes or Members for Business Pages and Groups respectively. If you begin with a Profile Page, it can be difficult to re-direct your audience to a Business Page if you reach the 5000 friends limit. For this reason, it is best to create a Business

---

17 Your social presence includes any existing social media accounts associated with your student organization. It also includes how you position your brand on social media.

Page or Group instead of a Profile Page for your organization. Be cognizant of this limitation when creating your Facebook presence.

If your structure is less of a brand and more of a community of people with a common interest, you might consider creating a Facebook Group instead of a Business Page. These are two very different structures and should be carefully reviewed to ensure you are using Facebook to your most effective advantage.[18] See Figure 9.3 for a comparison of key differences between Business Pages, Groups, and Profile Pages.

Facebook Business Page	Facebook Group	Facebook Profile Page
Optimized for brands	Optimized for communities	Optimized for personal connections
Can tag Business Pages	Can tag Business Pages; Facebook Groups, and Profile Pages	Can tag Business Pages; Facebook Groups, and Profile Pages
Facebook Ads and Analytics available after 30 Likes	Facebook Ads or Analytics not available	Facebook Ads or Analytics not available
Fans Like the Page. No limit to # of Likes	Fans are Members of the Group. No limit to # of Members.	Limited to 5000 Friends
Admins are the faces of the brand	Admins are members like everyone else	You are like your Friends
Fans are not alerted by new activity	Members are alerted by new activity	Tagged activity is shared on your Timeline; Non-tagged activity is shared on your Newsfeed
Admins interact with fans as Page	Everyone interacts personally	Everyone interacts personally
Conversations based around content generated by the brand	Conversations based around topics generated by the members	Conversations based around topics generated by you and Friends

Figure 9.3: Comparison between Facebook Business Pages, Groups, and Profile Pages

The Tag Function. Photo sharing can be very valuable due to the tagging function. It is important to note the tagging limitation for Business Pages. If you have a Business Page, and you post a photo, you can only tag that photo

---

18 Loomer, J. (2012, August 31). How to Leverage Facebook Groups. Retrieved April 20, 2016, from http://www.jonloomer.com.

with other Business Pages, not Groups, or Profile Pages. This is something to keep in mind when attempting to tag speakers in photos on your Business Page. If they have Business Pages, it is possible; otherwise, it is not. However, if you change your post status from admin to visitor, you will be able to tag other Profile Pages or Groups on your Business Page.

The "@" Function. You can tag Business Pages, Groups, and Profile Pages in text format in your posts by using the "@" function. When you type the "@" symbol in the post field, you will see a list of profiles pop up with names spelled the way you type. For example, if you type "@U," you may see a list of companies whose names start with a "U." The more characters you type, the more specific your list becomes until you find the exact entity you seek. When you find it, click on it, and it will be added to your post. Once published, the post will be seen on both your timeline and from the newsfeed or timeline associated with the tagged entity. This is great for pointing others to different locations on Facebook, and for increasing exposure and market reach.[19]

9.4.3 TWITTER

Twitter is a form of micro-blogging and is great for sharing links. Its profile simplicity makes it very easy to set up and manage. Due to the 140-character limitation, you should consider ways to maximize the impact of the limited amount of characters in your tweet. Some ways to do this are as follows:

The "@" Function. When including "@" in a tweet, write something directly after it with no spaces, and you will see a list of existing profiles with usernames spelled the way you are typing. From that list, you can select one of the corresponding user handles, and it will be added to your tweet. When you draft and submit your tweet, the profile manager of the handle you included in your tweet will be notified and in doing so may have a higher probability of responding. A favorable response is a Retweet (RT). You can usually help increase the probability of an RT by submitting a tweet with a user handle and a Thank You or some other form of appreciation for their services because

---

19   It may not always be necessary to include the @ symbol in order to trigger a list of usernames.

you are a fan or any number of other reasons why you might give thanks to someone or something. Give value to receive value.

Hashtags (#). The hashtag was organically created by Twitter users and was initially done to more easily find tweets. The search function in Twitter now allows for the recovery of tweets with searched words regardless of whether or not a hashtag was used. In this capacity, it is better to use the hashtag less for indexing and more as a way of driving follower participation and brand engagement much like how Coca-Cola did with its #MakeItHappy campaign.[20] Hashtags should be used to invite the audience to take some form of action. This may be by way of sharing content, replying to and Retweeting. All of these things help increase brand exposure.

URL Shortener Programs. URLs can use up a lot of characters in your tweet. Use one of the following programs to shorten your URLs:

* **Bitly**
* **Goo.gl**: Available as an Extension for Chrome

9.4.4 BUILDING A PRESENCE FOR YOUR CAMPAIGN

When your student organization markets an event on social media, you can strengthen the impact of your campaign by inviting all your board members to market the event via their own social media profiles. Create and use a hashtag for the event or set of events and use that when publishing posts to quickly retrieve tweets associated with your event(s). Encourage board members to interact on social media and have a presence. This will help enhance your reach and strengthen market awareness of your event(s).

9.4.5 USING SOCIAL MEDIA TOOLS

With the advent of new technology comes a wealth of tools and applications to augment your workflow. The following is a list of some of the many tools that help compliment your social media strategy.

---

20 Lee Yohn, D. (2015, February 18). Use Hashtags to Generate Greater Brand Engagement. Retrieved April 20, 2016, from http://www.forbes.com.

* **HootSuite**: Social media dashboard
* **TweetDeck**: Twitter dashboard
* **Facebook Insights**: Facebook analytics[21]
* **Google Analytics**: Popular analytics tool offered by Google
* **Google Alerts**: Monitor the web for content. This is a great social monitoring tool for listening to what is being said about you or your business.

9.4.6 IMPLEMENTING YOUR STRATEGY

In online marketing, you have three goals: strengthen relationships with existing customers; find new customers; and increase conversion rates. For student organizations, these three goals include: strengthening relationships with existing members; finding new members; and increasing the number of RSVPs to your events. The more members you have, the better the chance of increasing the number of RSVPs when marketing your events. In social media, the same logic applies. The more followers you have, the more likely you are to increase conversion rates when sharing links to squeeze pages.[22]

While not entirely effective, it is common practice to create a social media page and then invite friends to follow it. The problem with this method is your friends may or may not be an accurate representation of your target market. If they are not, your follower base will be made up of artificially inflated demand for your product or service offering. To avoid this situation and create a more robustly targeted consumer base, strategically place your product or service in front of those individuals who are more likely to buy what you are selling. The key term here is Target Market. Identify it, find it and attract it.

> Target Market: Identify it, find it and attract it.

---

21 Facebook Insights are accessible to Facebook Business Pages that receive at least 30 Likes.

22 This can be assumed as long as your focus is on providing honest value to your target market.

With a simple Google search, you can find an almost endless amount of content about social media strategy. Here are a few classic strategies:

Strategy #1: **Social Media Advertising**[23]
LinkedIn, Facebook, and Twitter allow users to promote their pages or products on their platforms for a fee. Each one also allows you to select your desired targeting parameters. Your ads will only be visible to the audience that possesses characteristics indicated within your parameters. If done correctly, you have a strong chance of gaining significant traction with new users.

In one occurrence, an advertisement for a Facebook Business Page received over 1000 Likes in under 12 hours. See Figure 9.4 for a screenshot of the analytics for that ad.[24]

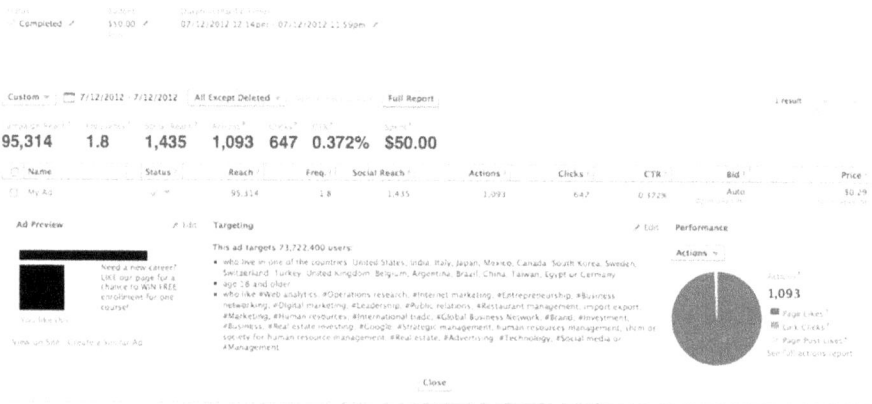

Screenshot used with permission.
Figure 9.4: Facebook Ad Analytics

This ad ran from 12:14 pm to 11:59 pm on July 12, 2012, and attracted 1,093 new Page Likes. The ad targeted over 73 million Facebook users 18 or older, from 18 different countries, who had any one of the various keywords in their profiles that were included in the parameters. The ad text started with

---

23 In July 2012, I created and implemented the Facebook advertising campaign discussed in this section.

24 The title and photo are blacked out to ensure privacy.

a question and followed with a call to action. Specific key words were capitalized to generate attention. The price for this ad was $50. So for $50, the ad ran for just under 12 hours and attracted 1,093 new customers.[25]

Before creating this ad, the target audience was identified of the business affiliated with the associated Facebook Business Page. Demographics such as age, location, and interests were reviewed. The ad was positioned around these characteristics to strategically place it in front of the prospective customers with the highest likelihood of becoming converts. As you can see, this was a very effective advertising strategy.[26]

While the goal of the above advertisement was to increase the number of Likes to the associated Facebook Business Page, another strategy could be to re-position the ad so it points to a squeeze page. The squeeze page redirect is a great strategy for building your email list if you are selling an information product either as a developer or an affiliate.

Strategy #2: **Offer Temporary Free Usage**

If you can offer value, consider providing opportunities where your users can interact with your product free of charge. For student organizations, this may be in the form of allowing prospective members to attend some predetermined number of events before committing to membership.[27] This helps the non-member see the value first before committing to it.[28] In Internet marketing, this strategy is implemented with the intention of building trust with the audience. Once trust is formed, you are in a better position to up-sell and drive conversion rates.

The free offering should be a sample of the total product or service you can provide to the customer. For example, let's say you have an eBook that is 150 pages, and you want to sell it to an audience of prospective customers. One strategy would be to give away an outline to the eBook complete with brief

---

25 The $50 was a credit provided by a Facebook promotion so my ad was technically free.

26 Results may depend on brand recognition, market reach, and ad cost.

27 This number is decided at the discretion of the executive leadership of your student organization but emphasis should be placed on membership registration.

28 Marketing events exclusive to members helps drive additional interest from prospective members. This type of event might be something more significant than a general networking event, such as a conference or seminar.

descriptions of each chapter. Another strategy would be to give away chapter 1. If the customer wants to know more, they can purchase the full eBook for some predetermined price. On social media, you could share a link to an automated squeeze page with an opt-in page that requires the user to submit an email address to receive the free offering, which should be automatically sent to his or her email account as a PDF or some other electronic format.[29]

Strategy #3: **Run a Contest**

Contests have a way of driving awareness, traffic, and conversion rates. They also excite customers, which is a great benefit. If you run a student organization, ask your members to take pictures of themselves at your events and share them, while tagging your organization's profiles on their existing social media profiles. This will allow the photo to show up on your timeline as well as theirs. This will help drive "Likes" to the photo and get people talking, create buzz and hopefully make your campaign go viral. This will strengthen the visibility of your events. Using a random number generator program,[30] you will then randomly select one member who posted a photo to win something of value. This might include a book on a related topic or something else a student would find useful.

Apply this same strategy in business. The winning customer could be given a coupon that could be used toward the purchase of your product or service. In this way, the goal is to drive conversions. As stated previously, the more eyes you have on your product or service, the higher the likelihood of increasing conversions and making more money.

---

29 For a discussion on Opt-In Pages (Squeeze Pages), review section 9.3.3.3.

30 True Random Number Service. (n.d.). Retrieved April 20, 2016, from http://www.random. org.

SUMMARY AND APPLICATIONS TO ENTREPRENEURSHIP

Your marketing mix is critical to the success and longevity of your student organization. Marketing helps drive awareness of your product or service. Whichever medium you use to implement the drive to attract more eyes to your offering, it should be done with the intent to build trust with the consumer and drive conversion rates. The more eyes you have looking at your offering, the higher your chances are of increasing revenue. For student organizations, focus should be placed on increasing the number of students who attend your events. Common mediums for marketing your organization are: direct; word-of-mouth; print; email; and online. Consider each of these methods as important pieces to be integrated into your marketing mix and implemented on an on-going basis.

In business, focus your efforts on developing a quality product that you can use to capitalize on some market need. If your product is good enough, you may not need a marketing strategy as the product may just sell itself. If not, however, you will need to build your customer base. By creating and sharing free samples of your product with new and existing customers, you can strengthen relationships with your customers. Identify, find and attract your target market. Not everyone will buy your product so it is important to find and sell specifically to those who will. Your offerings should be authentic. Customers are smart and can usually spot nonsense when they see it. Once customers are aware of your product and find it useful in some way, they are more likely to talk about it with their networks. Good brands make money; great brands make money and create conversations.

Secret 10

BUILDING YOUR WEBSITE

This is the most technologically complex Secret. This Secret focuses specifically on the process of how to build and monetize a website for your student organization, or business. No matter what you do, you should strongly consider having a website. The website acts as an online portal where visitors can go to learn about and interact with your brand. This might include: registering for events, and/or purchase your product(s) and/or service(s). Routinely share links on your social networks that point to your website pages, especially when you are promoting an event, product or service with the specific intentions of monetizing and/or adding value. This is done to drive traffic and stimulate conversion rates. You should use your website to make money and/or add value. In this Secret, we will discuss how to do this.

For student organization leaders, see if an option exists for you to create a school-branded website for your organization and if so, investigate any existing associated limitations. If your academic institution offers a website template of some form, take advantage of it. If this option does not exist, we will cover the basic instructions on how to build a website yourself with minimal resource investment. Many student organizations are more focused on helping their members than on making money, which is normal and expected. However, monetization is covered here so you can see how a website can act as a revenue stream.

Web design consists of many different components, some requiring routine maintenance for the life of the website. A website is not something you create; it is something you do.[1] The content covered in this Secret includes: hosting companies; hosting plans; content management systems; file transfer protocol; managing plugins, extensions, and modules; managing website health; lean functionality; monetization; web advertising and keyword research; web analytics; and branding.

A website isn't something you create; it's something you do.

10.1 HOSTING COMPANIES

Before you design a website, you need a service that allows you to host your files so they can be viewed from an Internet browser. This service is called Hosting. Some of the activities you can do within your hosting account include: register and manage your domain(s); install web software; create users; and contact tech support. A quick Google search will turn up an extensive list of hosting companies. Here are some popular ones: BlueHost; DreamHost; GoDaddy; HostGator; MediaTemple; and NetworkSolutions.

10.2 HOSTING PLANS

Once you select a hosting service, you need to select a hosting plan. Be sure to familiarize yourself with the differences between Shared Hosting, Virtual Private Servers (VPSs), and Dedicated Hosting.[2]

---

1 A website is less of a noun and more of a verb.
2 Markle, B. (2015, December 2). Differences between Shared Hosting, VPS Hosting, and Dedicated Hosting. Retrieved April 20, 2016, from http://www.inmotionhosting.com.

10.2.1 UNDERSTANDING SHARED HOSTING

In a shared hosting plan, your files are stored on a server that shares resources with other users, which equates to a more affordable option. This is usually a great plan to start with because it offers enough power to operate your website without making a sizable financial commitment to resources you do not yet need. Your customization options are limited, and you share the maintenance cost as well as available resources with the other users on the server. While this may be a great option for smaller burgeoning websites, sites with more traffic and complexities may want to move to a Virtual Private Server (VPS).

10.2.2 UNDERSTANDING VIRTUAL PRIVATE SERVERS (VPSs)

In a virtual private server plan, you own and operate your own dedicated space. While some space is still shared with other users, it is much less. Because you have more space, you will enjoy a more efficient user experience. Your costs are higher, but your customization options are limitless. The VPS option is great for sites that generate a lot of traffic. If your site continues to grow and requires even more space, Dedicated Hosting may be a more suitable option.

10.2.3 UNDERSTANDING DEDICATED HOSTING

Dedicated hosting is the most expensive of the three hosting options stated here. In this plan, you are the only one on the server, and you have access to all available resources. Because you have your own space, you are free to use it however you wish.

10.3 UNDERSTANDING CONTENT MANAGEMENT SYSTEMS (CMSs)

A Content Management System (CMS) is a program that allows you to publish, edit, and modify content from a central admin interface. These programs can be used for many different kinds of web projects including but not limited to: blogs; image portfolios; ecommerce; and forums. Here is a list of some of the more popular CMSs, with an emphasis on WordPress.

10.3.1 USING WORDPRESS

There are two versions of WordPress and each caters to a unique audience. The version you select will likely depend on your technological competence and how you wish to operate your website. There is no wrong answer. Some users start with the *.com* variety and migrate to the *.org* version when they are ready to enjoy more customization options and manage more of the site on their own. The key differences between these two versions are listed in Figure 10.1.[3] Research the right version and then make your decision.[4]

WordPress.com	WordPress.org
Your website is hosted on servers owned by WordPress (fully hosted)	You host your website on your own server (self-hosted)
Security and backups are handled by WordPress, and optional upgrades are offered for a fee	You are responsible for securing a host, performing backups, and managing security
Install one of an extensive selection of free or paid themes	Install one of an extensive selection of free or paid themes, or build your own
Plugins are not supported	Install plugins to enhance feature functionality in many ways
Support forums: https://en.forums.wordpress.com	Support forums: https://wordpress.org/support

Figure 10.1: WordPress.com v. WordPress.org

If you are a novice to web development, WordPress.com might be right for you. It is very easy to set up and requires very little maintenance given that it is hosted on servers owned by WordPress. More annoying issues with security and updates are all handled for you. This leaves you stress-free to focus on creating and publishing quality content. The caveat to WordPress.com is that plugins are not supported. Plugins are developed to add valuable functionality to your site. These are only available on the self-hosted, WordPress.org platform.

WordPress.org allows for full creative freedom. You are responsible for updating, maintaining, and securing your site. You have the ability to install

---

3 WordPress.com and WordPress.org. (n.d.). Retrieved April 20, 2016, from https://en.support.wordpress.com.

4 Create beautiful sites with WordPress. (n.d.). Retrieved April 20, 2016, from http://get.wp.com.

plugins, and customize your theme to your liking with the ability to edit your theme's code. WordPress.org requires a bit of technical proficiency, so it is encouraged to have experience with web development. Some users build their sites on the WordPress.com platform, and then when they feel comfortable, they migrate their content to the WordPress.org platform.[5]

10.3.2 USING VBULLETIN

vBulletin is world-class community software. It allows you to create a robust forum environment. This is great for websites that want to gather communities for discussions about certain topics. vBulletin offers a range of nice options including mobile support and social integration. Fees are associated with licensure and upgrades.

10.3.3 USING OTHER CONTENT MANAGEMENT SYSTEMS

Some other popular CMSs include Drupal, Joomla, and phpBB. phpBB[6] is free, open source community software similar to vBulletin. This software comes with many options to enhance your site. This is great software if you want to build an online community without a significant financial commitment.

A variety of CMSs can be installed on your domain by using the One-Click Installs feature provided in many hosting dashboards. If you are unsure of where this is or if your host even provides one, inquire about this very handy feature. If your host does not provide it, you can simply download the necessary files from a CMS website, and upload them to your server via File Transfer Protocol (FTP).[7]

---

5 Greenough, P. D. (2016, March 26). How to Migrate from WordPress.com to WordPress.org. Retrieved April 20, 2016, from https://www.patrickgreenough.com.

6 Check with your host to see if this software is available as a One-Click Install.

7 File Transfer Protocol (FTP) is covered in section 10.5.

10.4 CONFIGURING EMAIL ADDRESSES

When you register a new domain name with your web host, you should create a unique email address to accompany the new domain. For example, ([you]@ [yourdomainname].com). Commonly used email address syntax for new domains include the following:

10.4.1 DOMAIN EMAIL ADDRESSES COMMONLY USED FOR BUSINESS:

* support@[yourdomainname].com
* [firstname]@[yourdomainname].com
* [lastname.firstname]@[yourdomainname].com
* [firstname.lastname]@[yourdomainname].com
* [firstinitialsandlastname]@[yourdomainname].com

10.4.2 DOMAIN EMAIL ADDRESSES COMMONLY USED FOR PROFESSIONAL ORGANIZATIONS:

* [title]@[yourdomainname].org – The login credentials can be shared if more than one person assumes the same role for an organization, i.e., Co-VP Programming, etc.

Most web hosts offer an email portal as part of their hosting package. This is where you can set emails up. You can also set up emails for your domain using Google Apps for Business. The per-title email address arrangement can be cumbersome for student and professional organizations so it might be more efficient to have a single designated email address to contact a point person in the organization, say the Secretary or VP of Communications to act as the communications liaison. The benefits to a single email address include: improved efficiency; stronger recall; consolidated email archiving; and officer transition streamlining. The email address itself could be info@[yourdomain-name].org.

10.5 UNDERSTANDING FILE TRANSFER PROTOCOL (FTP)

FTP is a network protocol used to transfer and edit files from host to host. This protocol requires user authentication for access privileges. Authentication data required to access FTP includes: host; username; password; and port. Familiarize yourself with the different file transfer protocols.[8] If you do not state which port you would like to use, it will default to port 21 (FTP), which means that both the command and data channels are unencrypted. If you indicate port 22 (SFTP), all data sent between the client and server is encrypted, which creates a safer access environment when using an unsecured network.

10.5.1 UNDERSTANDING FTP CLIENTS

There are many clients available for use to access your FTP files. It is important to consider your operating system when selecting an FTP client. Some are compatible with Mac only; some are compatible with PC only, and others are compatible with both. Here is a brief list of popular clients: CuteFTP; FileZilla; and FireFTP.

10.5.2 MANAGING USERS

You can create FTP users from within your host's admin dashboard. Locate the area called Users, or Manage Users and create a new user.[9] You need to state the Type of User Account, i.e., FTP, SFTP, or Shell. The differences are usually stated in the panel but if not you can always contact your host for clarification via phone, email, or Live Chat if that option exists. Next, you need to select a username and password. These are the same credentials you will use to authenticate with your FTP client. Once you have created a new user, you will need to assign it to a domain. This will allow you to access FTP with and only with these specific user credentials.

---

8 INFO: Secure FTP, FTP/SSL, SFTP, FTPS, FTP, SCP... What's the difference? (n.d.). Retrieved April 20, 2016, from http://www.rebex.net.

9 Investigate the location of this option in your hosting dashboard.

While not required, it is encouraged to create a new user for each domain you have. The default user created when you registered for an account with your host automatically has access to all domain files. By creating unique users for each domain, it enhances security when providing access credentials to a third party in the event you need assistance from another skilled professional. If you need to provide a third party with access to files from a single domain, the unique user access credentials will provide that person with access only to files on the respective domain without having access to or knowledge of files on your other domains if you have more than one.

10.6 UNDERSTANDING WEBSITE ADD-ONS

Most CMSs allow for rich customization options. This might include editing HTML, CSS, and PHP. Additionally, you are usually provided with options to enhance functionality by installing additional software add-ons. These add-ons have a unique name depending on the CMS you choose to use. Each of the top three most used CMSs uses a unique title for their add-ons: WordPress (Plugins); Drupal (Modules); and Joomla (Extensions).

No matter which CMS you use, managing these add-ons requires routine maintenance and careful observation. Before you install add-ons, make sure they are compatible with your version of the CMS. Depending on which CMS you use, this information may require a bit of research. If you use WordPress, this information is available by reviewing plugin details. This information will indicate if the plugin has or has not been tested with your version of WordPress. If it has been tested and is proven to work with your version of WordPress, install the plugin. If it has not been tested on your version of WordPress, install at your own risk.

If your website is working before you install the questionable plugin, note that before you install the plugin so that if anything changes, you will know the culprit is the incompatible plugin. If the plugin is not compatible or has not yet been tested on your version of WordPress, you may run into a series of issues such as 404 and Fatal Errors. Often when you receive error messages, they provide an indication as to where in the code the issue exists. If the error message does not provide this information, do the following to help get your website back online:

*   **Delete the plugin via FTP:** When you receive these error messages, you may be prevented from accessing your CMS dashboard. If this happens, log into your FTP client, delete the recently installed but outdated or incompatible plugin, then try logging back into your CMS dashboard. Usually, this fixes the issue if the cause of the error was the plugin.

10.7 MAINTAINING WEBSITE HEALTH

If your site gets hacked, visit Google Webmaster Tools. You will be given instructions on how to verify that you are the owner of the site. Select one of the available options to verify. Once verified, Google will provide a health status report for your site. From there, you can take the necessary steps to ameliorate any detected issues. See Figure 10.2 for a screenshot of the Google Webmaster Tools dashboard.

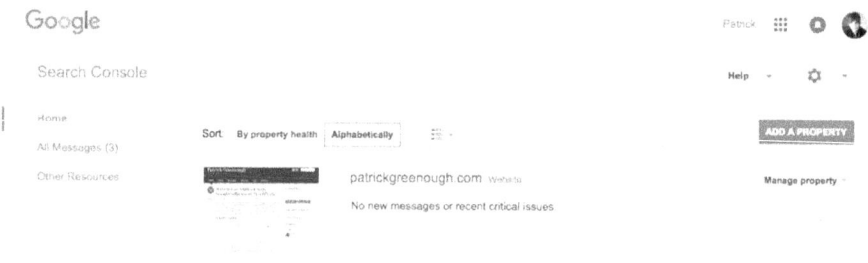

Google and the Google logo are registered trademarks
of Google Inc., used with permission.

Figure 10.2: Google Webmaster Tools Dashboard

10.7.1 AVOIDING SPAM BOTS AND SECURITY VULNERABILITIES

Due to the many variables associated with web development, you may run into a variety of other issues. Sometimes an incompatible plugin will attract undesirable robots designed by third parties, and intended to spam, or otherwise harm your site. This can happen with Subscription plugins that allow visitors to provide their email addresses to opt-in and receiving notifications of new information when it becomes available on your website. This action is desirable because it allows you to build your marketing communications list. However, you may also receive bogus email addresses created by spam bots, which can create problems.

Some hosts have specific rules associated with bounced emails. For example, if you publish a post on your website, it gets sent to your opt-in list. If your opt-in list is littered with spam email addresses, many of your messages will bounce. When this happens, and it exceeds the limit of bounced emails allowed as directed by your host, your host may shut your site down. The first step to fixing the issue is deactivating or deleting the Subscription plugin. This will prevent you from sending messages to bogus email addresses, but will also prevent you from sending messages to legitimate email addresses, which is the dilemma. From there you will need to research potential alternative Subscription plugins or other solutions.

10.7.2 KEEPING YOUR SOFTWARE UP-TO-DATE

Other problems may be created by outdated software. It is strongly encouraged to perform software updates as soon as they become available. Make sure you are operating on the latest version of your CMS and you are using the latest versions of compatible plugins. If you make this a habit, it will reduce the risk of security vulnerabilities. So be sure your software is up to date at all times.

10.8 LEAN FUNCTIONING

Add-ons are great for enhancing functionality on your website. Pay close attention, however, to how many and which ones you use or do not use. Install only those add-ons that you absolutely need to operate your website the way you wish. There are ways to get around using some plugins simply by changing the way you manage your site. For example, in the WordPress admin dashboard ([yourdomain].[root]/wp-admin), you can bypass the use of a spam prevention plugin by going to Settings > Discussion and inserting keywords found in spam comments into the Comment Blacklist field. Archive enough keywords in this field, and you should not need to install a spam prevention plugin.[10] Here is a list of keywords

---

10 If you're going to use a spam prevention plugin, Akismet is a popular option due to its reputation and reliability.

that were found in spam comments left on one of my websites. You can build your own list of blacklist words, or you can copy and paste the following list in Figure 10.3 right into your Comment Blacklist field to get you started.[11]

workout, dating, Louis Vuitton, weddings, sneakers, birthmark, backlinks, affiliate, oakley, shoes, weblog, bags, SEO, software, online, windows, shirts, pills, fashion, boots, ugg, sale, track, insurance, nj, traffic, youtu, AOL, kia, gamble, discount, mate, apple, ipod, autocad, station, hair, treatment, makeup, titanic, daily, kaution, gay, hotel, health, viagra, pharmacy, fb, storage, internet, computers, loans, payday, yob, opera, phone, airline, varta, nably, credit, betting, ads, zeit, life, divorce, html, club, porno, Nixon, crazy, shop, gold, dental

Figure 10.3: WordPress Comment Blacklist

Some plugins are necessary but be sure to investigate if there are other opportunities to manage your site without using a plugin first before performing installs. By using only the plugins you need and deleting the ones you do not, you can keep your site lean and free of unnecessary code and software. Much like a car, the fewer moving parts you have, the fewer problems you are likely to experience. The leaner your site, the better it will perform and the less likely you are to experience security breaches from malware often found on outdated or unused software. Malware can severely affect the performance of your site, and in some cases affect visitors' operating systems as well. Further, malware can even compromise your entire site and ruin or delete all of your data. Remember this one rule regarding website add-ons: If you don't need it, delete it.

Regarding website add-ons: If you don't need it, delete it.

Also, be aware of the changes your site undergoes when you perform regular software updates to your CMS. Sometimes, especially with WordPress, these updates will automatically install additional software on your website typically in the form of additional themes and plugins. These extra add-ons

---

11 Download the FREE template at https://www.patrickgreenough.com/resources.

can show up on your website several days after you perform an upgrade so be sure to keep an eye on your installs. While this extra software is automatically installed in inactive status, if you do not plan to use it, you should delete it. Keep your site as lean as possible and only use software you absolutely need to operate your website the way you want.

10.9 UNDERSTANDING MONETIZATION
10.9.1 UNDERSTANDING AFFILIATE MARKETING

A website is another income producing medium. Affiliate Marketing is the process of making a commission for generating conversions for a product or service owned by someone else. The following is a list of some of the popular income production and affiliate marketing programs you can use to monetize your website.

10.9.1.1 Google AdSense

Google AdSense allows you to deliver Google AdWords[12] ads to your website. The registration process may require you to input the following pieces of information.[13]

* **Email address and password**
* **Employee Identification Number (EIN):** This is required for annual tax filing.
* **Your business name:** DBA, or FBN
* **Business bank account name, number and routing number:** This will allow you to automatically get paid when visitors click on your ads.
* **Website URL**

Once your Google AdSense account is set up, you can design the look of the ad box. Each ad box is assigned a batch of automatically generated code

---

12 Google AdWords is covered in section 10.10.1.

13 For details on how to set up some of these items, refer to section 4.2.

that you can put on your website where you want the ad to be shown. This code will have unique identification information related to your account so you can get paid directly for clicks on ads.[14] The content of the ads is generated from keywords within content on your website. To ensure that ads are relevant, keep the content on your site as consistently relevant as possible.

10.9.1.2 *Amazon Associates*

Amazon Associates allows you to get paid for each conversion made when a visitor clicks through from your Amazon product links. If the user purchases a product while they are there, you will be paid a percentage of sales. This is a helpful resource if you run a product review site. Keep in mind, however, that search rankings can be negatively impacted if you include too many Amazon affiliate links on your home page.[15] Try to find a balance between the amounts of content and number of affiliate links. This is just something to keep in mind as you produce and place Amazon Affiliate links.

10.9.1.3 *eBay Partner Network*

eBay Partner Network is another popular affiliate marketing network. This program allows you to advertise eBay auctions. If someone clicks on an advertisement link and makes a purchase, you get paid.

10.9.1.4 *Other Popular Affiliate Networks*

- o ClickBank; ClixGalore; CommissionJunction; CommissionSoup; FlexOffers; JVZoo; LinkConnector; MaxBounty; NeverBlue; oneNetworkDirect; PeerFly; PepperjamNetwork; Rakuten Marketing, and ShareASale

---

14 You are strongly discouraged from clicking on your own ads. Let that be done by visitors.

15 Haws, S. (2013, March 13). How to Get a Google Penalty Using Affiliate Links (And How to Recover). Retrieved April 20, 2016, from http://www.nichepursuits.com.

     o   DataFeedr: WordPress plugin for building affiliate marketing niche websites.

10.9.2 UNDERSTANDING INFORMATION PRODUCT CREATION AND MARKETING

Creating and selling your own information product is a great way to augment your income potential. An information product is something typically offered in some electronic form and is meant to provide instructional value on some topic of general interest. Take, for example, an eBook on how to make money online. Great format examples of info products include: eBooks; video instructions; and audio recordings. By creating and selling your own info product online, you have a highly desirable opportunity to separate how you spend your time and how you make your money. To do this, you will need to focus on automating processes and finding others to market your product for you. Place is space with regard to your info product, and the merchants that market your product are called affiliates.

Affiliate marketing is a marketing strategy whereby Internet marketers are rewarded with some predetermined percentage of the per unit sale price when they stimulate conversions from their own marketing efforts. The number of affiliates can be positively correlated with target audience reach. While some amount of effort should be made on finding and approving your affiliates, it is not uncommon for the right affiliates to seek you out, thereby allowing you to direct your attention elsewhere. This arrangement qualifies as organically generated process flow efficiency.

Affiliate marketing improves marketing efficiency by allowing others to market your product for you. If you market your own product, you will only receive profits on your own per unit sales. If you have 100 affiliates marketing your product, and you give each affiliate a percentage of each per unit sale they drive, your income generation potential greatly increases. The example from section 9.3.4 is re-created here:

* Your email list size: 50,000
* Price point for your product: $97
* Conversion rate: 2%
* Total revenue: (50000 x .02) x $97 = **$97,000**

Now, let's say you have 100 affiliates, each with an email list size of 50,000 with a 70-30 profit sharing ratio, i.e., you give them 70% of each unit sale of $97, and the other 30% goes to you. The same math applies. They market your product to their lists and receive 2% conversion rates. Here's the formula:

* 97 x .7 = $67.90 (Reward given to each affiliate for each sale of your product they drive)
* 97000 x .7 = $67,900 (Reward given to a single affiliate for driving a 2% conversion rate with a product cost of $97 sent to a list of 50,000)
* 97 x .3 = $29.10 (Revenue you capture from each per unit sale generated by your affiliates)
* 97000 x .3 = $29,100 (Revenue you capture from a single affiliate for driving a 2% conversion rate with a product cost of $97 sent to a list of 50,000)
* $29,100 x 100 = **$2,910,000**

The equation above illustrates that if you provide a 70-30 profit sharing ratio for 100 affiliates, and each affiliate drives a 2% conversion rate with a product cost of $97 sent to a list of 50,000, you will make $2,910,000! This number will vary depending on the number of affiliates, their list sizes, their conversion rate percentages, product price point, and your profit sharing ratio. This is an example of the income generation potential associated with having affiliates market your product for you. This illustration also shows you how to separate how you spend your time and how you make your money.

> Focus on separating how you spend your time
> and how you make your money.

10.10 UNDERSTANDING WEB ADVERTISING & KEYWORD RESEARCH

Once your site is set up and you are providing quality content, your Google search rankings will partially depend on the level of relevance of the content and number of common search terms or keywords within your content. To improve your search rankings, you should consider keyword research. If you know what words people are using to search for content, you can include these keywords into your content to enhance your search rankings. Google provides a keyword tool called Keyword Planner as part of the Google AdWords package. To take advantage of this tool, you will need to sign up for a Google AdWords account.[16]

10.10.1 USING GOOGLE ADWORDS

AdWords is Google's advertising campaign creation tool. This program allows you to set a budget for advertising including how much you want to pay for each click on your ad. This practice is commonly referred to as Cost-Per-Click (CPC) and is part of your Pay-Per-Click (PPC) campaign. These ads are primarily focused on keywords. Users can create ads using keywords people commonly use when searching the Internet via Google. The commonly searched keywords trigger the ads to show up. In this way, it is important to consider your keyword choices carefully to enhance the effectiveness of your ads.[17]

10.10.2 USING GOOGLE KEYWORD PLANNER

Keyword Planner is connected to the AdWords package and is Google's keyword research tool. This is a powerful tool that offers a variety of unique keyword testing options and associated proposed budgets and bids. This can be very handy when planning an AdWords campaign. A simple Google search will reveal a variety of How-To information pieces so be sure to try this tool and learn to use it to your advantage.

10.11 GENERATING WEB ANALYTICS

When you have a website, you will want to know how visitors are interacting with it. Understanding visitor behavior can be valuable knowledge that can

---

16 As with other Google products, use your Gmail login credentials to sign up and log in.

17 This is a nutshell description. Exceptional proficiency in this strategy will require thorough research on Search Engine Optimization (SEO).

potentially help you enhance your online revenue stream. For example, let's say you discover more visitors are spending more time on one specific page than anywhere else on your website. You can leverage this action by providing rich content on that specific page. This might include articles, ads, product pitches, or anything else that may stimulate conversions.

10.11.1 USING GOOGLE ANALYTICS

Google Analytics is a service that provides detailed statistical information about web traffic, which includes behaviors and sources.[18] This service also measures conversions and sales data. When you are in the Google Analytics dashboard, add a property. When you add a property, you will be provided with a batch of code to include on the website associated with that property. This code is what enables statistical recording and tracking of your website analytics data. Depending on how your website is set up, where to integrate your Google Analytics code may vary. If you are operating a website in the WordPress environment, you can add this code to your website in two different ways:[19]

1. Add analytics code to the header.php file
2. Install the Google Analytics plugin

After you have added the Google Analytics code to your website using one of the above methods, you will be able to view web analytics associated with that particular website from your Google Analytics dashboard. This will allow you to review the data and plan your content delivery strategy accordingly.

10.12 WEB BRANDING

Your website should have its own unique brand. Pages and logos should be consistently displayed with regard to your desired brand identity. This section covers the website header logo and favicon. The header logo is that which is

---

18 As with other Google products, use your Gmail login credentials to sign up and log in.
19 Greenough, P. D. (2016, April 18). How to Add Google Analytics to Your WordPress Website. Retrieved April 20, 2016, from https://www.patrickgreenough.com.

often found on the top left corner of the home page of many websites. Some header logos are larger than others, and often called banners. Also, your website should have a small icon that browsers can display on web tabs when viewing your website. This small icon is called a favorites icon, or favicon for short. Both the banner and the favicon should be formatted and sized accordingly. Let's have a closer look at how to create your banner and favicon. One way to create these branded images is to design them in Photoshop.

10.12.1 CREATING YOUR BANNER

The banner is the branded image that you see displayed on the top left corner of the home page of many websites. It is the primary logo for the brand. It is usually dynamic in the sense that you can click on it at any time and from any page on the website and it will redirect you to the website's home page. The size of your banner is dependent on your preference but remember the bigger it is, the more real estate it will cover. If your goal is to make money with your website, it is in your best interest to save as much real estate on non-monetized content as possible. You do not need to shrink your banner to the size of your favicon, which we will discuss in the next section. However, you should be conservative when selecting the size of your banner.

If you are curious about the size of images being used on some websites, install Firebug on the Firefox web browser. Firebug is an element inspection tool that allows you to view software code associated with any element on any webpage. This means you can inspect various elements such as size dimensions and CMYK color tone numbers for anything on the Internet. It is a very handy tool for new and existing web developers.

10.12.2 CREATING YOUR FAVICON

The favicon is the small icon you see in a tab opened in your browser while viewing a website. The standard size of a favicon is 16p x 16p. You should always re-size your favicon to 16p x 16p before adding it to your website.[20]

---

20 Some responsive WordPress themes may require a larger size as a catchall for various displays.

This will help enhance the ease of display in web tabs when your site is viewed on any browser. The brand of the favicon should be consistent with the brand of the banner; it might even be the same. It is entirely up to you. No matter what you decide to do, make sure your brand remains consistent throughout the life span of your website.[21]

---

21 For a discussion on branding, refer to Secret 8.

SECRET 10: BUILDING YOUR WEBSITE

SUMMARY AND APPLICATIONS TO ENTREPRENEURSHIP

This Secret teaches the basics of web development. For student organization leaders, before tackling a web development project, first, investigate if your academic institution offers any branded website template options. If these exist, use them. If these options do not exist, the information provided in this Secret should help you get started on building your own website.

A website is something that all businesses should strongly consider having. Your website is your online brand. It is like a house; you want it to be inviting so people will want to stay longer. Much like a house, building a website requires strategic planning and answering a long list of complicated questions related to the development process. Building a website can be an overwhelming process, but it does not have to be. This Secret provides detailed instructions on how to build, manage, and monetize your website. It should act as a helpful reference guide for anyone new or experienced in the art of website development.

EPILOGUE

Creating and maintaining a student organization and identifying a viable monetization strategy are complex processes that require focused thinking and articulated planning. This is a helpful reference guide for building sustainable student organizations and how the process relates to starting businesses. The content in this book is primarily based on leadership, marketing, and technology.

Passion and success are positively correlated when accompanied with action. We are all fortunate to have the ability to introspect. While some of us may not know it, each of us possesses some skill that we can use in some way to advance the community in which we live. This statement does not just apply to using your skills to the advantage of others but to yourself as well. You should think of your skills and abilities as a way to actualize your own goals. Take a moment to ponder; think about your skills and abilities. Ask yourself the following questions:

* What skills and abilities do I possess from which others may benefit?
* How can I utilize these skills and abilities to reach my own personal goals?

After you have identified your skills and abilities, think about goal setting and attainment. Then ask yourself another series of questions:

*   What are my goals?
*   Is how I am spending my time bringing me closer to achieving them?
*   How do I want to spend my time in this lifetime?
*   What is my ideal lifestyle?

Spend some time thinking about the answers to these questions. Write down your skills and abilities. Then, next to each skill and ability, write a list of ways in which you can utilize those skills to bring you closer to achieving your goals.

It is important to identify your weaknesses but do not waste valuable time trying to improve them. Instead, focus on leveraging your strengths. Your strengths are what will have the richest and most efficient impact on your goal attainment strategies. Focus on going from good to great at least, instead of going from bad to mediocre at most.

Focus on going from good to great at least,
instead of going from bad to mediocre at most.

One final thought – it is all in your head, everything… Think about it. Everything you have done in your life has led you to this very moment right now. If you are not where you want to be or doing what you want to do with your time, think of what you can do right now to actualize your ideal lifestyle. When we are at the end of our lives, aside from uncontrollable variables, each one of us will have lived the life we ultimately wanted. Whether you want to live a meager and frugal existence or one rich with freedom to travel, live anywhere and do anything, **it is all up to you, everything…**

You are as successful as you want to be.

EPILOGUE

www.ingramcontent.com/pod-product-compliance
Lightning Source LLC
Chambersburg PA
CBHW050508210326
41521CB00011B/2369